FINISHING WELL

Establishing a Lasting Legacy

By
DR. RICHARD CLINTON and
DR. PAUL LEAVENWORTH

Convergence Publishing (2012)

Copyright © 2012 Richard Clinton and Paul Leavenworth

All rights reserved.

ISBN-10: 1479372110

EAN-13: 9781479372119

Table of Contents

About the Authors	v
Preface (Paul)	vii
Introduction (Paul)	xiii
Chapter 1: Finishing Well (Paul)	1
Chapter 2: Living With the End in Mind (Richard)	17
BARRIERS	
Chapter 3: Moral Barriers (Paul)	33
Chapter 4: Relational Barriers (Richard)	57
Chapter 5: Faith Barriers (Paul)	73
TRANSFORMATION	
Chapter 6: Deep Processing (Paul)	93
Chapter 7: Renewal (Richard)	111
Chapter 8: Focused Living for Convergence (Paul)	131
Chapter 9: Spiritual Authority (Richard)	145
LEGACY	
Chapter 10: Ultimate Contributions and Legacy (Richard)	165
Chapter 11: Passing the Baton (Paul)	183
Chapter 12: Afterglow (Paul)	197
Appendix (Paul)	215
Resources (Paul)	245
Bibliography (Paul)	249

About the Authors

Richard Clinton is currently the Senior Pastor of a Vineyard Church in Colorado Springs, CO. Before taking his current position he served in pastoral roles at other Vineyards in the U.S. and Switzerland. He has also served as an Adjunct Assistant Professor of Leadership at Fuller Theological Seminary (CA) and as the Director of Barnabas Resources, an organization committed to "equipping, training, and releasing effective leaders into service for the Kingdom of God."

Richard completed his undergraduate studies at Westmont College (CA) and his M.A., M.Div., and D.Min. at Fuller Theological Seminary. His father, Dr. J. Robert (Bobby) Clinton has recently retired after forty plus years as a Professor of Leadership in the School of Intercultural Studies at Fuller Seminary.

Over the past several years Richard and Bobby have co-ministered together in the area of leadership training and development while developing the Clinton Leadership Institute (www.jrclintoninstitute.com) to continue the process of Biblical research in leadership development.

Richard is married and has three sons. He currently lives in Monument, CO.

Paul Leavenworth is currently the Executive Director for the Convergence group (www.theconvergencegroup.org), a consulting organization committed to helping leaders finish well. Before taking his current position he served as the Executive Director for Leadership Development and Church Ministries for Open Bible Churches. He has also served as an instructor at Eugene Bible College (now New Hope Christian College), a missionary with YWAM, and a college administrator at Christian liberal arts colleges.

He completed his undergraduate studies at Oregon State University and has completed an M.A. in Theology at Fuller Theological Seminary. He has also completed a M.Ed. in Guidance and Counseling from Whitworth College (WA) and an Ed.D. in Counseling from the College of William and Mary (VA).

Paul is married and has three children and currently lives in West Des Moines, IA.

Preface

It is hard to believe that almost twenty years ago Richard Clinton and I (Paul Leavenworth) wrote *Starting Well: Building a Strong Foundation for a Lifetime of Ministry*. Our hope back in 1994 was to get an established publishing company to edit and publish our work. We felt that there was a need for Biblically based materials designed to help young emerging leaders establish a foundation of intimacy with God and integrity in life and ministry.

I still remember getting the rejection letters back from publishers. The letters went something like this,

"Good content... needs editing... we do not think there is a market for a book like this... Thanks, but no thanks!"

Richard and I were disappointed but convinced that there was a need (even if there was not a market) for a book like *Starting Well*. Both of us were in teaching situations at the time so we made copies of our rough draft and used the materials in our classes.

Fortunately, Richard's father, J. Robert Clinton, Professor of Leadership (now retired) at Fuller Seminary in Pasadena, CA, had established Barnabas Publishers (in his garage) to publish his research on Biblically based leadership development and offered to publish a thousand copies of *Starting Well* through Barnabas.

Little did we know at the time that over the years *Starting Well* would be translated in Spanish, German, Korean, and Indonesian and become a textbook in Bible colleges, seminaries, and other youth training programs (YWAM, Master's Commissions, etc.).

When Richard and I wrote *Starting Well*, I had a sense that we would be co-authoring two sequels, *Living and Leading Well* and *Finishing Well*, at some time in the future. Well, that time has come. Earlier in 2012, Richard and I completed an updated and expanded version of *Starting Well*. During our discussion about this project we sensed that it was time to write the sequels and complete what we call the Well Trilogy.

Finishing Well is the third and final book in our Well Trilogy. Our first book, *Starting Well*, focuses on spiritual formation and leadership development during the first ten years of ministry. *Living and Leading Well* focuses on navigating mid-life challenges that ministry and marketplace leaders face as the evaluate their spiritual and leadership formations for focused living and finishing well. *Finishing Well* focuses on establishing our legacy in our later years. *Finishing Well* gives the reader an opportunity to assess ultimate contributions while navigating necessary transitions in life and leadership in order to establish a lasting legacy.

Our Vision

Our vision in writing *Finishing Well* is to provide Biblically based insights, strategies, and resources for older, experienced leaders who are facing the inevitable transition from positional authority to spiritual authority (whether they minister in the context of the church, marketplace, or other social settings) as retirement and the issues related to getting "old" become more and more a reality.

We have co-authored this book because Richard and I are in the midst of learning how to navigate various stages of mid-life and we each bring unique life experience, ministry experience, and gifting to this project. We also believe that there is "synergy" in collaboration. Bobby mentored both Richard and me in his leadership development paradigm and each of us is attempting to apply his research findings in our own settings. Richard is navigating mid-life as a pastor of a local church. I am navigating the later stages of mid-life as I enter into semi-retirement in my early "senior" years as a consultant and coach helping leaders finish well.

We trust that through our collaboration there will be a greater perspective on critical aging issues that will connect with a greater spectrum of types of people. Each of us has authored individual chapters based on our interests, expertise, and life experiences.

Our Goals

This project is designed to integrate Biblical leadership principles, lessons, and examples with real life experiences to help the reader to understand the dynamics and challenges of growing older and navigating the end game in such a way that they do not hinder God's ultimate purposes for their lives. To put it simply, our goal is to help older (50-60s) men and women who have started well, lived and lead well to finish well and leave a lasting legacy for God's glory, their fulfillment, and the next generations benefit!

Richard and I write from a two-fold bias: 1. A Male perspective, for obvious reasons, and 2. A Ministry perspective, because that is where we have primarily served. We believe that the following material is applicable for men and women who serve in ministry and the marketplace, but some of you may have to work a little harder to understand our language.

With this in mind, we believe that there are Biblical principles that can be understood and applied that can help us to start, live and lead, and finish well. Our focus in this book is on **finishing well**. The goals of this project include:

1. To provide an overview of the leadership "landscape" of getting older so that we can anticipate challenges and opportunities in order to cooperate with God in his purposes.

The Introduction will introduce you to J. Robert Clinton's Leadership Emergence Theory (LET). This leadership development stage theory is the baseline for all of our Well Trilogy. *Finishing Well* focuses on the convergence and afterglow life stages while giving opportunity for the reader to become more focused and intentional on fulfilling God's purpose through your unique role and methodologies, in order to establish a lasting legacy as you finish well in life and leadership.

Chapter 1: Few Leaders Finish Well will describe the reality that "few leaders finish well." Many who do not finish well are taken out in mid-life because of flaws in their character that are exposed by the challenges, pressures, and crossroads of this critical stage of life. For older leaders, plateauing can be a subtle barrier to finishing well.

Chapter 2: Living With the End in Mind will describe the big picture in terms of destiny processing and how we can enter into the fullness of God's purpose for our lives in a focused and intentional manner. Knowing something about where we are going can be very helpful as we attempt to finish well and leave a lasting legacy.

2. To provide Biblical insight and opportunities to examine your spiritual formation foundation as they relate to moral, relational, and faith barriers that if not dealt with can lead to burnout, blowout, or plateauing.

Part 1: BARRIERS will give you an opportunity to examine and evaluate your spiritual formation foundation relating to barriers to finishing well caused by unfinished business related to moral, relational, and faith issues in your life and leadership.

Chapter 3: Moral Barriers will expose you to the three primary moral barriers to finishing well: sexual immorality (Samson - Judges 13-16), misuse of finances (Judas - Matthew 26, John 13), and abuse of power (Saul - I Samuel 18-19).

Chapter 4: Relational Barriers will describe for you the three primary relational barriers to finishing well: family issues, wrongful pride, and emotional wounding.

Preface

Chapter 5: Faith Barriers will introduce you to the two primary faith barriers to finishing well: plateauing (Gideon – Judges 6-8) and boundaries (Thomas – John 20-21).

3. To minister to your inner life as well as provide information about convergence and afterglow as you prepare to finish well and establish your lasting legacy.

Part 2: TRANSFORMATION will focus on the ways in which we cooperate with God as he initiates a deeper relationship with him through difficult times so that we become more aware of his calling and become more focused and intentional in purposes for our lives, leadership, and legacy.

Chapter 6: Deep Processing will describe for you the process and purposes of enduring in grace through the really hard situations of life and leadership. As we learn to rely more completely on God, regardless of life's circumstances, we can appropriate God's resources for bearing much fruit.

Chapter 7: Renewal will give you information and practical life application insights to find God's renewing resources so that you will be able to persevere over the long haul of life and leadership.

Chapter 8: Focused Living for Convergence will introduce you to the four focal points of a focused life: unique purpose, unique role, unique methodologies, and ultimate contributions. We can gain greater and greater clarity about these issues as we learn consistency in our obedience and as we mature personally and as leaders.

Chapter 9: Spiritual Authority will describe what spiritual authority is and its importance for finishing well in life and leadership and establish our lasting legacy. Spiritual authority is the primary influence base for kingdom impact in ministry. Spiritual authority flows out of humility and brokenness.

4. To provide Biblical and real life insights and examples for navigating the challenges and embracing the opportunities of end game growth and ministry.

Part 3: LEGACY will focus on how we establish a lasting legacy. Ultimate contributions will be defined and described in this section as well as the key transition from positional influence to relational empowering. Passing the baton to your successor is critical to how you finish and what your legacy will be. Afterglow offers tremendous opportunities to relationally empower the next generation of leaders.

Chapter 10: Ultimate Contributions and Legacy will define and describe twelve ultimate contributions and how they connect with your lasting legacy. Understanding ultimate contributions can help you become more focused and intentional in your calling and strategic in how you spend your time, use your gift mix, and use your resources as you near the finish line of life and leadership.

Chapter 11: Passing the Baton will describe the importance of healthy transitions as an older leader prepares, coaches, and serves the successor so that there is as little confusion, conflict, and collateral damage as possible. How you leave a position speaks volumes about who you are and how well you will finish.

Chapter 12: Afterglow will describe some of the significant opportunities that seasoned leaders have to empower the next generation of leaders. The older leader has time, flexibility, and wisdom that can be leveraged into significant mentoring, coaching, teaching, and consulting opportunities.

It is our desire that *Finishing Well* will be a blessing to you. How our life and leadership ends, how we make critical transitions to empower the next generation of leaders, and the quality of relationships we have will determine how we finish and the quality of our legacy. We trust that God will meet you in the pages of this book and that your "strength will be renewed" and that you will better be able to "fight the good fight" so that someday you will stand before God and hear, "Well done... good and faithful servant!"

Introduction

It is the "heart" of our leadership that really matters and Jesus is the gold standard by which true leadership must be evaluated and ultimately lived out. J. Robert Clinton (*The Making of a Leader*) has studied leadership from a Bible-centered perspective for four plus decades. From his studies, Clinton (p. 14) has developed the following definition of Biblical leadership:

> "Leadership is a dynamic process in which a man or woman with God-given capacity and God-given responsibility influences a specific group of God's people toward God's purpose for that group."

A closer look at this definition reveals that there are two *inputs* leading to two *outputs*:

1. God-given capacity

2. God-given responsibility

INFLUENCES

1. God's people

2. God's purposes

The inputs of Biblical leadership involve God-given: 1. capacity and 2. responsibility. All leaders have capacity and responsibility to influence. Capacity involves personality, life experiences, social networks, and gift mix (natural abilities, acquired skills, and spiritual gifts). These capacities can and need to be developed and maximized in the context of God's grace, because God will hold us responsible for what we do with what he has given us (see Matthew 25: 14-30).

The purpose of Biblical leadership is to partner with God in his purpose(s) to INFLUENCE others by the power of the spirit and word. *The outputs of Biblical leadership* involve: 1. God's people and 2. God's purpose(s). All people are God's people - believers and non-believers. As Bible-centered leaders we need to figure out whom it is that God wants us to influence (and for what purpose). This is usually a process of discovery which Clinton calls the "little-big" principle, "Whoever can be trusted with very little can also be trusted with much..." (Matthew 16: 10, NIV). This process of discovery and growth usually involves the following principles:

1. God develops a leader over a lifetime.
2. All leaders are disciples, but not all disciples are leaders.
3. God sovereignly uses people, circumstances and ministry assignments to shape the life of the leader.
4. Effective ministry comes out of a "being" relationship with God.
5. If we obey God's will, we will grow in character and influence. If we do not obey God's will, we will stagnate in character and influence.
6. Mature leadership involves an integration of spiritual formation, ministry formation, and strategic formation:

* *Spiritual Formation* – emphasis on developing intimacy with God and integrity.
* *Ministry Formation* – emphasis on identifying and developing gift mix (spiritual gifts, natural abilities, and acquired skills).
* *Strategic Formation* – emphasis on understanding and developing God's call and unique philosophy of ministry, and being intentional about accomplishing it.

The basis of kingdom influence is that "effective ministry comes out of healthy relationships with God and others" (Clinton).

Introduction

That is why character is addressed so thoroughly in both the Old and New Testaments as "essential" for effective leadership. Paul describes the qualifying characteristics of church leaders in I Timothy 3: 2-7 and Titus 1: 6-9 as they relate to choosing elders for leadership in the church.

J. Robert Clinton has based his leadership studies on the exhortation in Hebrews 13: 7 that says, "Remember your leaders, who spoke the word of God to you. Consider the outcome of their way of life and imitate their faith" (NIV). Clinton has developed his leadership emergence theory (LET), a stage theory, out of his years of studying Biblical, historical, and contemporary leaders in multiple cultures and gender roles. He and his students at Fuller Seminary have case studies of over four thousand Biblical, historical, and contemporary leaders representing men and women from diverse social and cultural circumstances to verify this theory.

LET involves six stages (see Diagram 1) that build on one another as the Christian grows and matures towards fulfillment of God's ultimate purpose for his or her life. Each stage is unique in its focus and forms the basis for advancement and effectiveness in the next stage. Each stage involves processing unique God ordained circumstances in ways that lead to growth of character, maturity, and expansion of ministry.

Diagram I: General Time Line

General Time Line

Stage 1	Stage 2	Stage 3	Stage 4	Stage 5	Stage 6
Sovereign Foundations	Inner-life Growth	Ministry/Leadership Maturing	Life Maturing	Convergence	After Glow

Each of these stages provides unique challenges and opportunities to experience God in deeper ways and to grow and mature as disciples and leaders. This model of leadership development emphasizes both character (being) and competency (doing) development.

We can either cooperate with God in these circumstances that lead to growth in character, maturity, and effectiveness; or we can resist God and stagnate in our growth and development as leaders. Three basic elements are involved in the process:

1. God initiates development throughout a lifetime so that we will become more Christ-like.
2. We can respond positively or negatively to God's sovereign initiation in our life.
3. If we respond positively, we grow in Christ-like character, maturity, effectiveness, and influence; but if we respond negatively, we will stagnate until we respond positively to the issue.

These three elements form the basis for our growth, maturity, effectiveness, and influence as we progress from stage to stage in our development as Christian leaders. There is no guarantee that we will progress in our leadership development through all six stages. But it is God's intention that each one of us realizes our full potential as we grow in maturity. He has given us his son, his word, his spirit, the church, as well as a host of Biblical, historical, and contemporary examples to rely on and learn from. He wants us to learn to appropriate all that he has done for us and given us so that we might "run with perseverance the race marked out for us" (see Hebrews 12:1-3). Let's take a brief look at each of these six stages of leadership development.

Stage 1 - Sovereign Foundations

The first stage is called sovereign foundations. This stage involves God's sovereign laying of a foundation for a person's life through

Introduction

his or her family, social, and historical context. God places each of us in a relational and historical context that will maximize our opportunities to know him and to become the person whom he desires us to become. God's sovereign involvement in the foundational aspects of our birth, race, gender, family, culture, and historical context is described in Psalm 139: 13-16:

> "For you created my inmost being; you knit me together in my mother's womb. I praise you because I am fearfully and wonderfully made; your works are wonderful, I know that full well. My frame was not hidden from you when I was made in the secret place. When I was woven together in the depths of the earth, your eyes saw my unformed body. All the days ordained for me were written in your book before one of them came to be."

God knows us! He knows everything about us. He knows of our self-centeredness and what it will take to bring us to him. He allows us to be exposed to the devastating consequences of sin in our lives, relationships, societies, and world affairs so that we will recognize our need for him. Paul describes the nature of sinful humanity in the following passage:

> "There is no one righteous, not even one; there is no one who understands, no one who seeks God. All have turned away, they have together become worthless; there is no one who does good, not even one. Their throats are open graves; their tongues practice deceit. The poison viper is on their lips. Their mouths are full of cursing and bitterness. Their feet are swift to shed blood; ruin and misery mark their ways, and the way of peace they do not know. There is no fear of God before their eyes." (Romans 3: 11-18, NIV)

He also gives us ample opportunities to know him. Even in cultures where the gospel has not yet been proclaimed, God has given a witness in creation and conscience (Romans 1:20). But in cultures such as ours, he has also given us the Bible and the witness of the church. If those who have not been exposed to the gospel are without excuse, how much more are we responsible to God for his witness to us?

Not only does God know what it will take to bring us to him, he loves us (see John 3:16) and knows of our potential to love him and become all that he has destined us to be. Each of us has a destiny to have a love relationship with God and to fulfill a specially designed role in God's plan to save a lost humanity from their sin.

The reality of God's sovereignty in these foundational matters is not meant to diminish the tragedy and heartache of broken relationships or inhumanity. God does not allow any circumstances to take place in our lives that he has not faced on our behalf (see Hebrews 4:15-16) and that he cannot use for good (see Romans 8:28). Human heartache and tragedy can become the context for growth and blessing.

Stage 2 - Inner-Life Growth

The second stage is called inner-life growth. This stage involves developing a foundational relationship with God out of which Christ-like character and maturity develop. During inner-life growth we make our initial commitment to Christ as Savior and Lord and begin to learn to relate to him in a process of life transformation.

The development of a devotional life (not a just a "time") is critical during this stage. We will want to spend time with this person who loves us so much that he gave his life that we might be set free from the bondage of our sin.

Love is a powerful reality. If you have ever been in love, been around some one in love, or wished you were in love; you know that people in love want to spend time with each other, do things with each other, and do things for each other. When we receive a letter, e-mail, text, or phone call from our loved one, we drop everything in order to see or hear what they have to say. When our behavior is displeasing to our loved one, we try to change it. This is the reality of our new relationship with Christ, our loved one.

The importance of an intimate relationship with God based in a healthy devotional life is well documented in Biblical, historical, and contemporary leaders who have started, stayed, and finished well. Out of our growing relationship with God will come God initiated opportunities for the transformation of our character from being self-centered to Christ-centered. God initiates this process in the inner-life growth stage in three primary areas. These areas include integrity, obedience, and word checks:

- *Integrity checks* are special tests that God initiates to reveal the true intentions of our heart and when passed serve as a springboard for the expansion of a person's capacity to be trusted by God.

- *Obedience checks* are special tests that reveal our willingness to obey God regardless of circumstances and apparent consequences and when passed lead to the realization of God's promises.

- *Word checks* are special tests that reveal the ability to receive and understand a word from God, and allow God to work out the fulfillment of this word.

Stage 3 – Ministry/Leadership Maturing

The third stage is called ministry/leadership maturing. This stage involves developing and maturing in effective leadership through the identification and application of one's gift mix and ministry/leadership skills. This process can take place in vocational, lay ministry, and/or marketplace contexts where one can be challenged to respond positively to leadership tasks, relationships, conflicts, and authority. It is in this initial phase of ministry/leadership involvement that a person begins to discover their gift mix.

A person's gift mix is made up of a combination of spiritual gifts, natural abilities, and acquired skills. It is through the obedient (and loving) use of your gift mix that you will probably have your most rewarding and influential opportunities to impact others. Leadership skills refer to those specific skills that you acquire in leadership situations that help you to perform tasks more effectively.

An awareness of your gift mix is important, but it is in the context of leadership opportunities, ministry tasks, relationships, conflict, and submission to authority that you learn how to effectively lead and minister. Loving relationships with God and others is a priority in this stage. To accomplish a task in an unloving manner is not mature leadership. Love is the baseline for effective leadership. God's plans must always be accomplished God's way!

Stage 4 - Life Maturing

The fourth stage of development is life maturing. This stage involves developing a personal sense of calling (for a closer look at calling see Appendix D: Strategic Formation) and a mature Biblical philosophy of ministry/leadership. We will take a brief look at philosophy of ministry/leadership here.

A personal and mature Biblical philosophy of ministry/leadership is foundational for convergence in stage 5 when inner-life preparation, a person's giftedness, ministry/leadership experience, and philosophy come together in the effective and fruitful expression of one's destiny or ultimate purpose. Ministry/leadership philosophy refers to the ideas, values, and principles that a Christian uses for decision-making, for exercising influence, and for evaluating personal, relational, and ministry effectiveness.

Introduction

The process of developing a personal philosophy of ministry/leadership involves three factors and three sub-stages (Table 1). The first factor is the Biblical dynamic. The basis of any mature philosophy must be the Bible. The second factor is our personal giftedness. We tend to see life and ministry/leadership through the grid of our giftedness. And the third factor is our personal experience. We tend to see reality from our own experience. Neither our giftedness or experience should contradict the Bible, but they will play a significant role in the development of our ministry/leadership philosophy.

Table I – Characteristics of Ministry/Leadership Philosophy

Factors	Sub-Stages
Biblical Dynamics	Osmosis
Personal Gift Mix	Baby Steps
Personal Experience	Maturity

Ministry/leadership philosophy develops over time. We have a philosophy in earlier stages, but it is not usually personal or mature. Ministry/leadership philosophy usually develops through the three sub-stages of osmosis, baby steps, and maturity. Osmosis refers to the beginning stages of developing a philosophy when we learn primarily by observation of others and by experimentation. We are attracted to someone's ministry or leadership so we try to minister just like that person. We read a book or go to a seminar and try to implement what we learned in our own situation.

The next sub-stage after osmosis is called baby steps. In the baby step sub-stage we learn by intentional design and evaluation. We begin to seek God for Biblical principles for life and leadership and evaluate our performance on this basis. We begin to ask questions about whether traditional or contemporary ways of doing things are necessarily God's ways. We are beginning to find our own sense of purpose, role, methodologies, and contributions.

The final sub-stage is maturity. In this stage, Christian leaders are able to articulate their philosophy in terms of lifestyle. Ministry/leadership philosophy is no longer theory - it is now practical and forms the basis for decision-making, exercising influence, and evaluation. Along with this there are also four major lessons that need to be learned during this stage if we are to move on to convergence:

1. Mature ministry/leadership flows out of mature character.

2. Mature character is formed through obedience in difficult situations.

3. Many Christians go through difficult situations without knowing of their potential benefits. It is important to discover God in the midst of difficult situations and learn of his grace.

4. Mature leaders operate with spiritual authority as their primary base of power. In this development phase, leaders learn how spiritual authority is cultivated. In essence, spiritual authority is not a goal but a byproduct of obedience. Obedience in the difficult seasons of life leads to a depth of Godly character that facilitates spiritual authority.

Stage 5: Convergence

The fifth stage of development is convergence. This stage involves the mature coming together of inner-life preparation, ministry/leadership maturing, and life maturing to fulfill one's calling, destiny, or ultimate purpose.

Introduction

Convergence involves the coming together of five major and five minor factors. The major factors include dependence upon God, giftedness, ministry philosophy, role, and influence. The minor factors include our experience, focus, methodology, destiny, and legacy (see Table 2). In convergence, the leader has the sense that things have come together in such a way that he or she is operating at the maximum potential in leadership that God desires for him or her. I call this "supernatural natural" living!

Convergence involves the substantial realization of our full potential as God's beloved children and co-workers in several areas that are essential for our fulfillment as healthy and whole human beings. These include the following major and minor factors mentioned above:

Table 2 – Characteristics of Convergence Stage

Major Factors	Minor Factors
Dependence on God	Life Experience
Giftedness	Focus
Ministry Philosophy	Methodology
The Right Role	Destiny
Appropriate Influence	Legacy

Stage 6 – Afterglow

The final stage is afterglow. This stage is characterized by the enjoyment and influence available to a person who has substantially completed their life calling or destiny. This stage is rarely attained (in part because so few finish well), but when convergence has been realized and God grants additional years to a Christian leader they can continue to have a major influence through their relationship with others. The primary tasks in this stage are to finish well and pass the baton of leadership on to the next generation.

Spiritual mentoring can be a major influence role during this stage and have a profound impact on younger leaders. The establishing of a lasting legacy through the mentoring of others is very important in afterglow. This is a stage in which a Christian leader is able to enjoy the blessings of finishing well. From this status come strategic opportunities to encourage and influence the next generations of leaders.

A basic understanding of Clinton's leadership emergence theory will serve as the framework for the following chapters. The focus of this book will be on the later stages of life and leadership development: convergence and afterglow, but we will also make reference to the prior stages because of their ongoing importance for developing our spiritual formation foundation. Remember, cracks in our foundation begin to become more noticeable in mid-life and unless we address them we may find ourselves burning out, blowing out, or plateauing. Just because we "make it through" mid-life does not mean that we will finish well. We still have some major challenges facing us in the end game.

This book is designed to help you build upon your strong foundations, which have stood the weight and pressures of mid-life, so that you can become more focused, intentional, and strategic as you prepare yourself to finish well and establish a lasting legacy.

Chapter 1

Finishing Well

Finishing well in life and leadership is the desire of all well-meaning Christian leaders. We want to know that our life has had meaning and that our leadership has been helpful to others. But, unfortunately, not all Christian leaders finish well.

In fact, a leadership study of 100 Bible leaders revealed that one out of four finished well in life and ministry (Clinton, "Listen Up Leaders! Forewarned is Forearmed!"). Clinton discovered that only 11 of the 100 finished well, while there was not enough information to determine how another 14 finished – so, somewhere between 1 in 10 and 1 in 4 Bible leaders finished well. Unfortunately, historical and contemporary leaders have not fared much better!

What a wake up call this is! Just because you start "fast" in your Christian life does not mean that you will finish well. Remember, it is "not by might, not by power, but by my Spirit, says the Lord

Almighty" (Zechariah 4: 6, NIV). In our enthusiasm for our newfound relationship with God we can get pretty excited and even zealous. But that alone is not enough to make it to the finish line. That takes another dynamic called "discipleship," or what Eugene Peterson calls a "long obedience." So, what does it mean to finish well? What are we talking about here? Clinton defines finishing well as:

> "At the end of a person's life, they have a vibrant, growing relationship with Christ, and they have essentially fulfilled their calling and left behind a legacy of righteousness [for generations to come]." (Clinton, *Leaders on Leadership*, Barna (editor), p. 152)

Before we describe the components, barriers, and characteristics of finishing well, let's take a look at a few stories of folks who did not finish well. The tragedy of unfulfilled potential and the negative impact on those they lead should get our attention and reinforce the importance of finishing well.

First, let's take a look at a Biblical leader who failed to finish well. A case study of King Solomon reveals someone who started well, but over the long haul faded into immorality and ineffectiveness.

Solomon – Started Well, Finished Badly!

Solomon was the son of King David and Bathsheba (II Samuel 12: 24). He grew up in a dysfunctional family and became king after his father's death (I Kings 2: 1 and 12). Solomon had an early encounter with God at Gibeon (I Kings 3: 5) where God appears to him in a dream and granted him whatever he wanted. Solomon chose "wisdom" (KJV) or "discernment" (NIV). God was pleased with Solomon's choice (I Kings 3: 10-14) and granted him riches and honor as well. Great start - or is it?

Two insights emerge from a closer look at the text: 1. Solomon had already begun to make political alliances through marriage to foreign women (I Kings 3: 1); and 2. God warned Solomon that the impact of his wisdom, riches, and honor were based on obedience (I Kings 3: 14).

As we will learn from this study on finishing well, obedience is critical. God is merciful, gracious, forgiving, slow to anger, and much more, but there is also the reality that "a man reaps what he sows" (Galatians 6: 7, NIV). The reaping may not happen right away, but sooner or later we reap what we sow!

This is the case in Solomon's life. In Deuteronomy 17: 14-20 we are given an interesting insight into how the king was to conduct his life:

1. He was to read the Law all the days of his life so that he would learn to revere God, live obediently, and not view himself as superior to others (verses 18-20);

2. He was not to acquire great numbers of horses (verse 16);

3. He was not to take many wives so that "his heart will be lead astray" (verse 17a); and

4. He must not accumulate large amounts of silver and gold (verse 17b).

Solomon must have known this passage, especially because of the example and influence of his father David. He must have observed both the positive and negative ramifications of David's obedience and disobedience (see I Kings 2: 1-4). Although Solomon seemed to start well there were issues of the heart that he failed to deal with that eventually caused him to become compromised in all four of the requirements for kings mentioned above.

This does not mean that God did not use Solomon significantly. He did! Solomon built the temple in obedience to God (I Kings 6). The glory of God was manifested at the completion of the building and the start of worship there (I Kings 8: 10-11). Solomon was sought out for counsel by world leaders (I Kings 10: 1-13 and 24). He became extremely wealthy and prominent, but not all was well with him.

God appears to Solomon a second time after the completion of the Temple and again reminds him of the importance of obedience (see I Kings 9: 1-9). At this point in his life he has completed two major building projects: the Temple that took seven years (I Kings 6: 38b) and his palace that took thirteen years to complete (I Kings 7: 1). In the original scrolls these two statements run together and stand as an interesting contrast (especially in light of the decline of Solomon after the completion of the Temple).

Finally, Solomon's disobedience catches up with him. God eventually becomes angry with Solomon because his heart had turned away from God (I Kings 11: 9-13). From this time on, we see a pattern of adversaries, rebellion, decline, and eventual division (after his death). How did this happen?

Remember our four requirements for kings? Let's see how Solomon did. Was he obedient or disobedient?

- Horses – "Solomon had four thousand stalls for chariot horses, and twelve thousand horses" (I Kings 4: 26, NIV).

- Wives – "He had seven hundred wives of royal birth and three hundred concubines, and his wives lead him astray" (I Kings 11: 3, NIV).

- Gold – "The weight of the gold that Solomon received yearly was 666 talents..." (I Kings 10: 14, NIV)

Oops! Somewhere Solomon got off course. He either forgot that he was to read the Law all the days of his life and obey its teaching or he did it and thought somehow that its teaching did not relate to him. Either way he missed it BIG TIME and the consequences were devastating.

After Solomon's death his son Rehoboam became king (I Kings 11: 42-43); rejected the advise of the elders (I Kings 12: 8); increased the "yoke" on the people (I Kings 12: 11) which resulted in civil unrest (I Kings 12: 20-21); idolatry (I Kings 12: 25-33); division of the nation and ongoing conflict (I Kings 14: 30). What a mess!

Fred – Looked Good, Blew Out!

Let's now take a look at a fictitious Christian leader that I have compiled from my files. I will call him Fred (but he could be any of us). Fred grew up in a Christian home and made a commitment to Christ as a young person. He was a good student, involved in leadership at school and church, and aspired to be a pastor. He attended a Christian college where he was an honor student and student body president his senior year. He dated Betty from his sophomore year on and they were married after he graduated.

He had many great offers to be a youth pastor, but decided that he wanted to try and start his own church. He and his new wife moved to a location that they felt God was leading them to, got jobs, and started connecting with people. Fred had a big vision to grow a church that would impact the entire community of tens of thousands for Christ. He and his wife believed that such a vision had to start with prayer so they gave themselves to prayer and fasting as the foundation for their future church. Little by little others joined this prayer group until their small apartment living room was over crowded.

Fast-forward about twenty years. Fred and his wife are still in the same city. They now have two children and are pastoring a church of several thousand. Fred's vision is being fulfilled and his community is being impacted dramatically. He has gained a certain celebrity status among the greater Christian community in North America and beyond because of the growth of the church, its impact in the community, and his growing involvement in politics.

Fred wrote several best sellers, hosted large conferences, developed a network of churches, and even was appointed president of a large evangelical organization that was active on the political front. Christian leaders and even the President of the United States were now consulting him. Everything Fred touched seemed to prosper.

But there was another story being written. Fred had a secret life that he hated but could not seem to find freedom from. For months (probably years) he struggled to get control over a moral issue in his life. He would have times of victory and then fall back into its control. He felt trapped by his success – so many idealized him, but in his honest moments he knew that he was weak and was afraid that he would disappoint his followers.

This feeling of being trapped put even greater pressure on Fred and he found himself turning to his secret life for temporary release and comfort. Now he found himself acting out in ways that he never thought he would. He knew in the back of his mind that if he did not get victory soon that he might be exposed, but he was trapped. Who do you talk to who could understand and keep confidence? He was so ashamed, but there was momentum in his ministry. Some really good things were happening!

You can guess what happened – Fred was unable to find victory and the support he needed and eventually was found out with devastating consequences for himself, his wife and family, his followers, and the cause of Christ. What a mess!

Both of these case studies reveal the tragedy of lost potential and devastating consequences. They show us the heartache, disappointment, and devastation that come with leadership failure. But it does not have to be this way! We are all "one banana peel away from slipping and falling" (to quote a mentor friend of mine), but the Bible also promises us that we can be "more than conquerors through him [Jesus] who loved us" (Romans 8: 37).

This book is designed to humbly look at what the Bible has to say about finishing well through learning to "abide" in Christ (John 15: 5, KJV) and bear "much fruit." It is our heart's cry that more of us finish well in life and ministry for the glory of God, the expansion of his kingdom, our own fulfillment, and our lasting legacy.

Finishing Well

Remember Clinton's definition of finishing well? This definition has six components:

1. They maintained a *vibrant relationship with God* to the end;

2. They maintained a *learning posture* throughout life;

3. They modeled *Christ-like character* through the fruit of the Spirit throughout life;

4. They lived their lives in such a way that their *convictions and the promises of God were seen to be real* in their lives and ministries;

5. They left behind one or more *ultimate contributions or a lasting legacy*; and

6. They lived their lives with a *growing sense of destiny and made the necessary sacrifices to realize this* to a significant degree.

Not all the leaders who finished well had all of these components fully developed in their lives, but they all had many or most of them. They learned over the long haul how to depend on God to provide the strength to run the race with endurance.

From this definition, Clinton has identified seven characteristics of those who finish well. This list is helpful for us, as we become Bible-centered, spirit empowered leaders. It gives us a road map or GPS perspective on the types of qualities that we need to incorporate into our lives if we want to finish well.

1. **They had a *long-term perspective* on life and ministry.** These leaders understood that every decision matters. There are no short cuts! God sees our every action (and attitude), and every action (and attitude) will have consequences.

If you do not get caught when you act selfishly (sin) it is not because you got away with it, or that God is too busy on other things, or that he does not care. It is because of God's mercy. He is "compassionate and gracious, slow to anger, abounding in love" (Psalms 103: 8, NIV).

God wants to have a loving relationship with us where we learn to trust that he really has our best interests in mind. His ways are really better than our ways. Jesus reflected this in his words and actions when he said: "Yet not as I will, but as you will" (Matthew 26: 39, NIV). We can gradually gain his perspective on our lives and realize that his ways are really better than our ways.

2. **They had expectancy and periodic experiences of *personal renewal*.** These leaders understood the "depravation" process that God uses to expand our foundations (Matthew 7: 24-27), force our roots to grow deeper (Psalms 1: 3), or prune our braches to make us more fruitful (John 15: 1-2).

The depravation process allows us to gain deeper, more mature, understandings of God and how he works in and through us. Remember Jesus promises:

> "Ask and it will be given to you; seek and you will find; knock and the door will be opened to you. For everyone who asks receives; he who seeks finds; and to him who knocks, the door will be opened." Luke 11: 9-10, NIV

Do you see what is happening here? The Greek tense for the verbs "ask… seek… knock" is a present active imperative, meaning "ask, and keep on asking;" "seek, and keep on seeking," and "knock, and keep on knocking." This is a command of ongoing application. What happens here is that we receive and gain greater capacity to receive in the future. We find and gain greater capacity to find in the future; and the door is opened and we gain a greater capacity to walk through other doors in the future.

This is another example of the "little, big" principle. Those who are trustworthy in small matters are prepared to be trustworthy in larger matters (Luke 16: 10). In this process, God will meet us and renew our capacity to know him in deeper and more gracious ways.

3. **They practiced *spiritual disciplines* as a means of developing and maintaining intimacy with God.** Those who finished well understood that the spiritual disciplines were access points to intimacy with God and integrity. They understood the necessity of "dying to selfishness," and embraced this process through learning to submit to God through practicing spiritual disciplines.

Jesus told his disciples that, "anyone who does not carry his cross and follow me cannot be my disciple" (Luke 14: 27, NIV). Practicing spiritual disciplines is one application of this concept. As we draw closer to God through Bible study, meditation, prayer and fasting, etc. we encounter a holy God who reveals our selfishness so that we can submit to him and be set free.

Establishing the gracious discipline of practicing spiritual disciplines may be difficult at first (and at other times, especially if God is revealing new layers of selfishness), but it is an absolute necessity for the maturing Bible-centered, spirit empowered leader. The spiritual disciplines serve as connecting points for abiding (intimacy). Remember, "No branch can bear fruit by itself; it must remain in the vine" (John 15: 4, NIV).

4. **They had a *learning posture* throughout life.** These folks understood that life is a journey toward finishing well. They never completely arrived at their ultimate destination in this life (although they made progress). They understood that they "were

aliens and strangers on earth" (Hebrews 11: 13). The author of Hebrews says of Abraham, "by faith, he made his home in the promised land like a **stranger in a foreign land**" because "he was looking forward to a city with foundations, whose architect and builder is God" (Hebrews 11: 9-10, NIV, **bold** added; also see Revelation 21: 1-4 for further insight into the city that Abraham was looking forward to).

We never arrive in this life. The righteous live by faith (not formula). Those who finished well understood that today's faithfulness is the prerequisite for tomorrow's challenges. They learned not to put life on cruise control. Every day was an opportunity to be challenged in order to trust God in new ways and to grow personally and as a leader.

5. They were *accountable to others* in mentoring relationships. They understood that no one makes it alone. We need one another. Paul exhorts believers to "carry each other's burdens, and in this way [we] will fulfill the law of Christ" (Galatians 6: 2, NIV).

The "law of Christ" has at least two applications. First, the great commandment:

> "'Love the Lord your God with all your heart and with all your soul and with all your mind.' This is the first and greatest commandment. 'And the second is like it: Love your neighbor as yourself.' All the Law and the Prophets hang on these two commandments." Matthew 22: 37-40, NIV

There is more to this. Jesus told his disciples just before he was crucified:

> "My command is this: Love each other as I have loved you. Greater love has no one than this, that he lay down his life for his friends... This is my command: Love each other." John 15: 12-13, 17, NIV

Why would Jesus emphasize loving God, loving our neighbor, and loving each other if it was not important? We need one another. It is part of God's "very good" creation when he formed human beings in his own "likeness" (Genesis 1-2). We are social creatures who need loving relationships to be healthy and whole.

There is another important aspect to this that the folks who finished well understood. As "fallen" and selfish human beings, we all have blind spots and are prone (especially when under pressure) to act selfishly. Having loving friends in our lives that can tell us the truth about ourselves in appropriate ways can save us from making some really bad decisions (if we are open and teachable). Those who finished well had accountable relationships as safe guards to their vulnerabilities.

6. They invested significantly in the *next generation* through mentoring relationships. Those who finished well invested significantly in younger emerging leaders. They understood the importance of the "parental" blessing on the younger generation in order for them to realize grace to pursue God's purposes for their generation (which usually looks a lot different than his purposes for the older generation). The prophet Malachi put it this way:

> "Remember the law of my servant Moses, the decrees and laws I gave him at Horeb for all Israel. See, I will send you the prophet Elijah [or "the spirit of Elijah"] before that great and dreadful day of the Lord comes. He will turn the hearts of the fathers to their children, and the hearts of the children to their fathers; or else I will come and strike the land with a curse." Malachi 4: 4-6, NIV

There are two outcomes that are possible between the generations: blessing or cursing. Those who finished well understood this and they intentionally chose to bless (even though they might not have completely understood the next generation).

They also understood that by blessing the next generation, they were blessed. The Apostle John says it best: "I have no greater joy than to hear that my children are walking in the truth" (III John 4, NIV). This "mutual" blessing results in freedom for the next generation to pursue God in their own way rather than having to try to prove to the older generation that they are "right."

7. They ordered their lives and ministries in a *focused* way in order to accomplish God's calling. Those who finished well figured out their calling and focused their life's resources (time, energy, money, etc.) on faithfully hitting the "bull's eye." They had a growing sense of purpose and became intentional about ordering their lives in such a way as to realize this purpose.

Some in the Bible encountered God in dramatic ways, which revealed their calling. Peter (Matthew 16: 18) and Paul (Acts 9: 15-19) received dramatic callings, but that is not the norm Biblically. Most of those who finished well (as well as others) received their calling gradually through the "little, big" principle.

Abraham, for example, encountered God several times over a number of years. Each encounter gave Abraham greater insight into the specific aspects of his calling. Eventually, as Abraham learned to live by faith, God fulfilled his purpose for Abraham (see Genesis 12: 1-3) through the birth of Isaac (and Isaac's eventual marriage and fathering of a son).

The bottom line is that if we learn to be faithful, we will not miss God's calling and will gradually order our lives in such a way that we will fulfill it. Remember, we can be "confident of this, that he who began a good work in [us] will carry it on to completion until the day of Christ Jesus" (Philippians 1: 6, NIV). God is more committed to us finishing well than we are. If we are faithful over the long haul, we will finish well and hear, "Well done, good and faithful servant!" (Matthew 25: 21, NIV).

Barriers to Finishing Well

With so few leaders finishing well, the logical question is, "Why?" What is it that causes folks to not finish well? Clinton studied the lives of those who did not finish well and discovered eight primary barriers. For our purposes here we will categorize these in three groups based on the root cause of the barrier: moral, relational, and faith barriers.

Moral Barriers:
1. *Sexual immorality* – Samson (Judges 13-16)
2. *Misuse of finances* – Judas (Matthew 26, John 13)
3. *Abuse of power* – Saul (I Samuel 18-19)

Relational Barriers:
4. *Problems with marriage and family* - David (II Samuel 11-19)
5. *Self-centered pride* – Solomon (I Kings 3-11)
6. *Emotional wounding* – Jonah (Jonah 1-4)

Faith Barriers:
7. *Life and ministry plateauing* – Gideon (Judges 6-8)
8. *Boundaries* – Thomas (John 20-21)

In each of these cases, the person gradually "gave in" to the sins that ultimately brought him down. Sin is like cancer - it keeps growing until it kills, unless it is killed. It is "kill or be killed!"

The Bible gives us insight here. Sin (*haramtia*) means, "to miss the mark... a principle or source of action, or an inward element producing acts..." (Vine, *Expository Dictionary of New Testament Words*). The Bible reveals that sin is universal: "all have sinned..." (Romans 3: 23) and the only way to break its power is through confession (I John 1: 9), leading to repentance (see Jesus' gospel message in Matthew 4: 17).

Sin is a tricky reality because it appeals to our "fallen" nature. Sin promises much but delivers little. The Bible reveals that there is temporary pleasure in sin (Hebrews 11: 25), but it does not last or satisfy. In fact, it sets off a chain reaction that leads to guilt, shame, and even bondage (see II Corinthians 10: 3-5). Sin can be forgiven, but there may be severe consequences (see Galatians 6: 7-8).

It is best not to sin! And in Christ we "are more than conquerors" (see Romans 8: 28-39) and no longer are slaves to sin (see Romans 6: 15-23). We can say "no" to sin because Jesus said no to sin perfectly (see Hebrews 4: 15-16). We can establish righteousness in our lives and find freedom and satisfaction (see Matthew 5: 6). This may involve "spiritual warfare" (see Ephesians 6: 10-18) and is a winnable war because Jesus finished it on the cross (see John 19: 30) and he is even now making interceding for our victory in him (see Hebrews 7: 25).

In the chapters that follow we will describe in greater detail each of these barriers to finishing well with the hope that from examining them we can learn how to better navigate the challenges that we will face as leaders and be better positioned to finish well.

Application and Discussion Questions:

1. What does it mean to finish well in life and leadership?

2. What are the characteristics of those who have finished well?

3. What are the general barriers to finishing well?

4. What areas in your life do you need to address in order to be better prepared to finish well?

5. What kind of support and accountability do you have in your life?

6. Are you satisfied with where you are in life and leadership? If not, what are you going to do about it?

Chapter 2

Living With the End in Mind

Have you ever looked around a group of your peers and wondered... when did we all get so old? I (Richard) can remember a couple of years ago that I was in a mentoring meeting with a guy that I really enjoyed working with. I knew I was a "bit" older but I regarded him as a colleague. In the meeting, he was expressing his thanks for the mentoring and then dropped the line... "You are like a father to me". Fast forward a few more years and then I begin to hear the word "grandfather" creeping into conversations. My natural kids and my spiritual kids have begun to produce grandchildren and my role is changing. It happens to all of us, doesn't it? It feels a bit strange to be writing a book on finishing well when finishing seems so far away. At the same time, finishing is a lot closer than it used to be.

At any rate, if you are still in the game, you are to be congratulated! No matter how "old" you are or how many ministry years are under your belt, our hope is to provide you with some perspective and encouragement to finish well. As we have been sharing with you, most leaders don't make it this far. For a variety of reasons they have dropped out, blown up, or just stopped trying.

In this chapter, I want to give you an overview of what it means to be a leader in what we call "the end game". This term end game comes from the world of competitive chess. A chess game can be broken up into three parts that are simply called, the beginning game, the middle game, and the end game. Each part of the game has unique characteristics and each part of the game has different dynamics.

The game can be won or lost in each part. In other games, things can change very quickly and a heroic play at the end can win the game. In chess, each part of the game lays the foundation for the next part of the game. The connection between how we start and how the middle game goes is very strong. The middle game determines the end game. Pieces are lost and position is gained in each part of the game that determines how the rest of the game is played.

The same could be said about our leadership development. Using the chess game analogy for leadership development helps us to focus in on the special dynamics and characteristics of each season of development. Through all three of the Well Trilogy we have pointed out the challenges of each stage and have tried to give leaders perspective on how to navigate through them.

To be honest, none of us get it all correct. We don't do everything perfectly. We make mistakes. We make some poor choices. God covers most of them with his grace and mercy. There are some fatal mistakes that take leaders out. We have seen leaders who have overcome poor starts and bad choices in the beginning phases. This happens with leaders who understand humility, brokenness, and have a steep learning curve.

In the middle game, it is not as easy for God to overcome bad choices. Bad choices in the middle game carry consequences that can block leaders from moving into the end game. God's grace, mercy, and redeeming power can rescue leaders from bad choices in each phase of leadership development. God's heart and will is always pointed towards healing and redemption. But in terms of leadership development, our choices determine the direction of our development. For example, where should the end game for Moses have taken place? Was a mountaintop overlooking the Promised Land where Moses wanted to end up?

The Beginning Game – Starting Well

I want to quickly review the different phases of development that we have been describing in the previous two books in this series. Remember that we are describing general leadership development. We are describing tendencies and patterns. Each individual leader will develop in their own unique way. There are a variety of factors that determine their personal leadership development story.

When we write about the years that represent each phase of development, we are only speaking in generalities or averages. The beginning phases of leadership development are described in the first book, *Starting Well*, which covers the first 10 years or so of ministry. Our second book, *Living and Leading Well*, covers the middle phases of development - a time frame between 10 and 30 years. Our last book, *Finishing Well*, covers the end phases of development – a time frame that involves our last 10 to 20 years of life. Each leader will move through these phases at a different pace depending on many factors.

For example, a leader who begins to take leadership responsibility in a youth group context or university setting will face the beginning game in their late teens or in their early to mid 20's. The issues that they face, generally speaking, take a little longer to go through. The key issue in the rate of development is how fast they are learning the lessons that they need to make progress in their character development and the discovery of how to do ministry effectively. Leaders who start in this stage of life will have the longest middle phases.

A leader who comes to a Lordship decision later in life and assumes leadership responsibility in their 30's or 40's will generally move through the beginning phase a little quicker because life has already been preparing them for leadership. They are thrust into middle game leadership issues more quickly. The amount of time they have in the middle game will be shorter. It all depends on how the leader is responding to what is going on.

The way a person responds to what God is doing will make a big difference in the rate of their development. If they tend to recognize God's interaction more quickly and choose to respond to people and situations in a God honoring way, they will seem to move forward more quickly. If they struggle to recognize God's interaction with them or they do not choose God's way, it takes them a bit longer to learn the lessons and move forward in their development. *Just because a person gets older doesn't mean they are moving forward in their leadership development.* There are leaders who get "stuck" in their leadership development. They never make it out of phases because they either don't want to learn the lessons or they just don't get it.

So how does one know where they are in their own development? What is most important is to recognize what kinds of things God is doing and what kinds of lessons or values need to be learned in each development phase. There are markers, which signal a transition from one phase into the next.

Every leader begins their leadership development journey in the beginning phases. As I mentioned, this phase of development typically lasts about the first 10 years or so after a leader takes leadership responsibility. In this phase of development, the focus is centered on what God is doing IN the leader. Another way to say this is: God is more focused on what he is doing IN the leader than

THROUGH THE LEADER. Of course, the leader is doing ministry, but that is not the main focus.

There are a number of critical issues that are being worked on (from God's point of view). Of course, basic leadership character is being formed in them. Things such as the willingness to obey, the willingness to maintain integrity (including such important issues like faithfulness and truthfulness) and the willingness to be humble are the main character elements that are being formed into the leader.

Basic ministry skills are being formed in the leader. How to hear God's voice, how to pray, how to influence (lead) people, how to use the basic ministry tools (the Bible, communication, prayer) are being formed in them. Learning to work with a variety of different kinds of people and learning to resolve conflict is important. Learning to relate to authority in a God honoring way and learning to use God's authority in a way that honors him are also critical lessons that need to be learned.

The discovery of God's giftedness in a leader takes time. Ministry experience needs to be accrued and foundations need to be laid for building trust for the future. All of this is what is going on in the beginning phases.

God is working behind the scenes through the leader's network of relationships, their families, and the context of ministry that they are in. Most leaders speak about survival during this phase of development. They are dealing with the difference between what they expected ministry to be like with the actual realities of doing ministry. Dealing with disillusionment is one of the difficult challenges of making it through this phase of development.

The reality is that many leaders just don't make it through this challenging phase. There have been many studies done about what happens to seminary students in their first years of ministry. These studies suggest that nearly half of the graduates drop out of ministry in the first five years and experience some kind of burnout. It is not easy to navigate these troubling waters.

The Middle Game – Living and Leading Well

So what does it look like when a leader is moving out of the beginning phases into what we call the middle game? First of all, there are some clear characteristics that are visible. They have survived the treacherous waters of the first ten or so years of ministry. The leader is able to get ministry tasks done effectively. They have discovered their basic giftedness and are using it to get the job done. They have learned enough lessons in the relationship arenas to get through most conflict situations.

They have learned how to relate to authority above them without getting themselves in too much trouble. They have learned many lessons about how to use leadership authority. Many of these lessons were learned through tough situations, but nevertheless the lessons have been learned. They have learned how to recruit and attract people to what they are doing and are learning how to get people involved.

In the Western world or the more affluent parts of the world, there has often been a move towards vocational ministry.

They are getting paid to do ministry. In other parts of the world, they are not getting paid to do ministry, but are recognized by the groups of people they are leading as the leader and have leadership titles that describe their responsibilities. For leaders working in bi-vocational ministry settings, their leadership role in ministry is what their life centers on and how they earn money to live is secondary.

The shift between the beginning game to the middle game is not marked by clear events. This is true of most transitions in ministry. It is process oriented, more like a journey. The main feature in the transition is clarity about their life purpose. There is a sense that God has revealed to them their life purpose and they are moving toward it. They are moving towards accomplishing the tasks that flow from the life purpose. The sense of newness in ministry is long gone. It feels like they are now shifting to face issues about how to sustain and continue forward. The issues are now centered on things other than survival. The focus begins to shift on moving toward greater effectiveness.

In *Living and Leading Well*, we focused in on the specific challenges that face leaders in the middle game. Leadership development in this season of life is all about finding the right ministry roles that allow the leader to do what God has called them to do. This is a time to build on the foundations that were laid. It is a time when there is a maturing process going on in our faith. Usually, this maturing process is brought about by having to navigate a number of crises and problems that are part of normal life. There is also a maturing process in understanding one's giftedness and using it effectively.

Values that under-gird ministry philosophy begin to move from implicit to explicit. Ministry philosophy begins to emerge because the leader faces many ministry situations where they have to articulate why things are done the way they are done. Often it has to be defended and articulated in order to attract people to what God is doing. This forces ministry philosophy to be made explicit.

In addition to all of this, the leader faces a number of challenges. In Living *and Leading Well* we outlined the dangers of burnout, blowout, and plateauing. The social relationships are often the most difficult to deal with. The complexities of singleness or marriage and family have to be dealt with. The pressure on a leader is at its greatest during this phase of development.

There is a spiritual tendency during this phase that also can be problematic. There is the tendency in the middle game to start relying more on our own abilities, skills, knowledge, and experience and less on God as we do ministry. We do not have the same kind of dependency (and sometimes desperation) on God like we did in the beginning stages of ministry. We have accumulated some competency and can do things on our own. It is normally towards the end of the middle game that God begins to address this tendency. His goal is to move us back into a place of being centered on him and relying on him. Positively stated, there is a deepening and refreshing renewal in our inner life. On the negative side, this process often begins with some kind of breaking experiences where we realize our need for God.

Towards the end of the middle game, a prioritizing process emerges. Normally, some kind of focusing event happens which forces the leader to make clearer and clearer decisions about what they should focus on. The focusing event can be a sickness. It can be an accident. It can be a crisis. It does not have to be something so dramatic. It can be a tiredness of the routine and a growing desire for a fresh touch from God and a longing for a renewed sense of purpose in ministry. No matter what the focusing event is the end result is the same. The leader begins to say "yes" and "no" to ministry opportunities as they become more focused. This prioritizing process is one of the things that signals leaders that they are moving towards the end game.

The middle game is the longest of the three phases of leadership development. Leaders can be in this phase of development for up to 30 years. For example, let's assume that a leader lives a normal life span (75 to 80 years of age on average). If a leader enters ministry in their mid 20's and takes about ten years to get through the beginning phase of development, they are beginning to move in the middle game in their mid 30's. Around the late 50's or early 60' there is a kind of marker for transitioning into the end game. I suspect it is mostly psychological and social. It is around this age that most people start vocalizing thoughts and ideas about what is coming next in life. Everyone is unique so we can only speak in general terms. If this example were an average, that means the middle game would last around twenty-five years or so. That leaves the last ten to twenty years of life for us to focus on the end game.

The End Game – Finishing Well

When we talk about the end game in this book, we are talking about what is happening in leadership development in the last 15 to 20 years of life. As we have said before, God is working in our lives right up until the end. God continues to grow us and develop us all through our lives.

To be honest, the vast majority of our leadership research has been done on leaders who are in their beginning or middle phases of development. It has only been in the last few years that we have begun to focus our research efforts on the end game. We will continue to learn more and more in the next few years. What I am sharing with you about the end game in this chapter is what we have learned up to this point. My father, Dr. J. Robert Clinton, led a workshop recently where he began to share insights into the end game. In the workshop he presented his finding on end game ministry. Up to this point, he hasn't published these findings.

There are a number of key characteristics that mark the end game including a number of critical challenges that have to be negotiated. I want to point out again that few leaders make it to this phase of their leadership development. Every leader finishes, but the vast majority of leaders finish poorly because they are mired in issues that prevent them from moving into the end game. Some leaders get stuck in issues that trap them in the beginning or middle phases. They never make it to the part of leadership development that we are describing in this book. Few leaders finish well - a sad reality, but true.

For leaders moving into the end game, here are some of the special characteristics of this stage. The leader is moving into a time when they are operating in visible and tangible maturity in their ministry. They do ministry not only effectively (doing things well) but also efficiently (doing the right things well). They are making their maximum contribution to the kingdom at the end of the middle game and into the early part of the end game. Their life and ministry is focused.

Being focused means that they are living out the purposes for which God designed them. Their life purpose is clear and directs their decisions. In the middle game, they fashioned a ministry role that fits who they are and allows them to operate in their strengths and maximize their potential. This sets them up in the right networks and relationships that provide the context for their end game. They understand and have articulated their values and have an explicit ministry philosophy that explains their way of being in ministry and doing ministry. They are now moving into a special kind of focus in their lives and ministries. They recognize the end is coming and they want to leave something behind that honors God and is a testimony to a lifetime of ministry. Their lives are centered on doing the things that God designed them to do. They are experiencing the fulfillment of their destiny.

They are enjoying a special kind of leadership influence that comes near the end of a lifetime of serving. This influence finds expression in and operates through a lifetime of relationships and networks that have been established. They are able to utilize these networks to do ministry in ways that would not have been possible earlier.

Afterglow

In his workshop on Afterglow, my father has begun to break up the end game into two sub-phases. He calls one "pre-afterglow" and the other "afterglow". We are still in the process of figuring out exactly what belongs to these two sub-phases, but what we know at this time suggests that in "pre-afterglow" there is a shift from intense direct ministry into a season of ministry that is not as intense. There is a lot of activity that falls into the categories related to this transition. This is a time when some major ministry responsibilities are drawing to an end. There is a movement from lots of direct ministry (intimately connected to people) towards more indirect ministry (ministry through others and other indirect methods).

Often, the job description of the leader changes as room is made for the next generation of leaders to take their place. Often, the ministry job itself is phased out. And often, there is no more paycheck. This is often a clear signal that the shift between pre-afterglow and afterglow is happening.

A couple of years ago, I attended a week of meetings for the group of churches that I am a part of. Our national director was stepping down and retiring from this position. He served for a total of 12 years in this role. He began in his late 50's and was nearly 70 years old. One of the humorous moments at the meeting was when he showed a film clip from Monty Python's movie *The Holy Grail*. The scene was about two-guys who were collecting dead bodies to be disposed of later. One old guy was being carried on the shoulders of the one man that was collecting bodies. The old man kept yelling out "I'm not dead yet!"

Our national director shared that although he has stepping down, he is not dead yet and is looking forward to the next season of ministry. I chatted with him after one session and asked him what he was thinking of doing. He mentioned two things that were right in front of him. One, he wanted to go back to school and finish a doctorate that he had been working on and got interrupted by busy ministry. He also wants to write and finish some projects that he has wanted to work on. This is afterglow ministry.

Afterglow is a picture word—it takes us to a fire, which has burned down to a large set of glowing embers. Light and heat are still coming from this fire, which is in its finishing stages. Afterglow ministry refers to the latter stages of ministry when a Christian leader retires from his/her full-time Christian vocation or marketplace vocation and moves into a new season of effective ministry. Usually, the "retired" leader works with those who recognize his/her spiritual authority. They want to learn from the expertise that is represented by the years of ministry and leadership experience gained by this Christian leader. The transition into afterglow can take a period of time and be a little rocky.

Afterglow Activities

Paul will also comment in greater detail on afterglow activities, especially mentoring, in our final chapter (Chapter 12: Afterglow). For our purposes here, let me continue to paint the big picture of what afterglow and its activities are about. The kind of ministry activity that characterizes the end game and afterglow involves what my father calls consolidation. He defines it as, "The process of reinforcing a Christian leader's lifetime of ministry in the end game."

Focusing on and emphasizing the following kind of ministry activities accomplish this. In Clinton's seminar, he spoke about 8 miscellaneous kinds of things that leaders are involved in that help to consolidate what God has done through them. All eight of the ministry activities involve modeling. Modeling is deliberately sharing, exposing and living out the values, practices and priorities that have shaped a lifetime of ministry.

He described four of these afterglow ministry activities that focus on people and are relationally focused:

1. *Correspondence*: a deliberate increase in correspondence with the goal of sharing values and transferring ministry philosophy.

2. *Mentoring*: An increase in mentoring where significant time is invested in helping people.

3. *Sponsoring*: Increasingly (as one is able) to provide a sponsoring function that can include financial support and investing in future generations. This is a type of sponsoring that

is much needed as younger leaders face difficult transitions in their development and growth.

4. *Prayer*: And perhaps most importantly, leaders in afterglow have the opportunity to pray and spend time in intercession like never before.

There are also several organizational roles in which a leader in afterglow can flourish. He has seen two common endgame ministry activities related to organizations:

1. *Serving on boards*: Because of their experience and expertise, leaders in this stage of development are often asked to serve on leadership boards or leadership teams in various settings.

2. *Establishing foundations, trusts and fund raising*: Also, God can use leaders who have established a lifetime of networks and contacts to resources to start trust institutions and foundations which can sponsor and invest in ministries.

In addition to these ministry activities there are several other ministry opportunities for ministry in the end game. It requires a certain kind of person who is gifted in certain ways:

1. *Speaking ministry*: For those gifted to speak, leaders in afterglow are freed up to speak messages that contain their life messages and values that are critical to them.

2. *Writing*: For those gifted in written communication, there is time to reflect, write and articulate in various forms of written communication.

But there are challenges as well. The end game forces us to face issues that deal with what my dad calls limiting factors. In the end game, leaders do not have as much energy as they used to have. Every leader in the end game has to deal with limitations that are a part of the normal human aging process. As the human body ages, it just does not function as well as it did before. There are a variety of health concerns and issues that we have to face. Our mental faculties may not be as sharp as they once were. Our physical strength may not be as strong. Our ability to handle stress and pressure that was faced in the middle game comes back into play in these years. If we dealt with stress and pressure in unhealthy ways in the middle game, we are now living out the consequences of those decisions in the end game.

The complexities that families face can be a major challenge these days. These issues shape a lot of the reality that leaders have to face. Family systems are increasingly complex and the concept of nuclear families is not as common as it once was. The family has been under constant attack and under pressure for decades. Watching my own parents deal with me, my brother and two sisters' situations has been eye opening. The traditional role of what being a grandparent has blurred and new roles and definitions have to be worked out. This takes a lot of energy and can be very consuming.

In many parts of the world, financial realities can cause huge challenges. Because we are living longer and the cost of living and medical care are spiraling up and up, economic issues play an important role in the end game of leaders. These issues can cause a whole range of complications.

Yet in all this, leaders face many of the same challenges that every other leader has faced throughout history. It is the challenge of finishing well. As Paul wrote about in the first chapter, we know what a good finish looks like. We can see what the end of the race looks like. We have identified the goals and characteristics that make up a good end. None of the challenges that we face in the end game are impossible to overcome.

Most importantly, leaders who make it to the end game have already learned some valuable lessons along the way (or they would not have made it this far). They know that the most important ingredient for success in the life of a leader and in ministry is living, walking, breathing, and experiencing intimacy with God. The powerful presence of God surrounding us is the key. With God, all things are possible.

It is our prayer and hope that this book will inspire us, encourage us, and motivate us to abide in his presence right up until we see him face to face. It is our goal to address the issues that we face in the end game. In doing that, our highest goal is that you encounter the living God who promised us that he would walk with us every step of the way. As a friend of mine used to say every time a new challenge or problem popped up… "Richard remember, there is no panic in heaven! Not a problem for God. Find him and you will discover his solution already worked out long ago." Wise words! God knows how to help leaders finish well. He is deeply committed to it and he really wants us to finish well.

Application and Discussion Questions:

1. As you read through the overview of the beginning, middle and end game sections, where do you see yourself in your own journey?

2. What are the issues that you are facing in your "middle game" that you need to address before you move into the end game? Health issues? Emotional issues? Ministry wounds? Scar tissue?

3. What can you do now to better set up the end game scenarios that you want to experience?

4. When you review the major barriers to finishing well, which ones provide the most difficult challenges for you? Which ones do you have to fight against the most as you move into the end game?

Chapter 3

Moral Barriers

The Apostle Paul wrote about a war that goes on inside us between the spirit and the flesh:

> "So I say, live by the Spirit, and you will not gratify the desires of the sinful nature. For the sinful nature desires what is contrary to the Spirit, and the Spirit what is contrary to the sinful nature. They are in conflict with each other, so that you do not do what you want." Galatians 5: 16-17, NIV

Boy, can I (Paul) relate to this passage. There is a war going on in my heart and all around me. Two cartoons sum up my dilemma. The first is a *Pogo* strip and the sequence goes something like this:

Frame 1: "I have met the enemy…" Frame 2: "and it is me!"

The other is a *Farside* strip of two buck deer talking to each other during hunting season. Both have full racks of antlers and are standing on their rear legs facing each other. The one whose front you see has a bull's eye of his chest and the one whose back you see says to the other:

"Bummer of a birthmark, Hal!"

Both of these provide a humorous view of a couple of very important realities related to Christian leadership:

1. We tend to be our own worst enemies; and
2. The enemy attacks leaders knowing that if he can take them out he will discourage followers and denigrate their message.

These two realities make it incumbent upon the Christian leader to win the war over the flesh so that he/she can withstand the attacks of the enemy that will surely come (in one form or another).

In the next three chapters, Richard and I will take a closer look at major moral, relational, and faith barriers that have taken out many Biblical, historical, and contemporary leaders so that you can become more aware of these pitfalls and become proactive in defending yourselves.

Bobby and Richard Clinton (in Barna, editor, *Leaders on Leadership*) have identified eight major barriers to finishing well. There are certainly others, but these are major barriers that have emerged again and again in the failures of Biblical, historical, and contemporary leaders. I will address the three moral barriers to finishing well in this chapter:

1. *Sexual immorality* – Samson (Judges 13-16)
2. *Misuse of finances* – Judas (Matthew 26, John 13)
3. *Abuse of power* – Saul (I Samuel 18-19)

Let's take a look at each one of these separately and then I will make some general observations about the moral vulnerability of leaders in order for us to be better prepared to resist the temptations that are inevitable in life and leadership. First, let's take a look at the barrier of sexual immorality.

1. Sexual Immorality

If there is a number one barrier for men it is probably this one. In their book *Pastors at Greater Risk*, H.B. London and Neil Wiseman share these alarming statistics about pastors:

- 20% of pastors say they view pornography at least once a month.

- 49% of pastors say they spend less than 5 hours a week on the Internet while nearly 30% spend 5-10 hours a week on the Internet.

- 20% of pastors admit to having had an affair while in the ministry.

- 12% of pastors say that since they've been in ministry, they've had sexual intercourse with someone other than their spouse.

- 51% of pastors say that Internet pornography is a possible temptation for them; 37% admit that it is currently a struggle.

- 33% of the clergy and 36% of laity have visited a sexually explicit website (53% of the clergy and 44% of laity say they have visited sites a few times in the past year).

- 18% of clergy say they visit sexually explicit websites between a couple times a month and more than once a week.

- According to Focus on the Family's Pastoral Ministries Division, approximately 20% of the monthly calls to their pastoral care line deal with sexual misconduct and pornography.

Although this book was published in 2003, I am pretty sure that things have not changed much for the better. We live in a sexually charged society with easy access to just about anything. The "if it feels good, do it" sexual revolution of the 60s is now having some devastating effects on marriages, children, and our society. Philip Jenkins, in his book *Decade of Nightmares*, says of the ramifications of the 60s counter-culture sexual revolution:

> "Sexual mores changed not just in terms of private behavior but also in public discussion and display. The new frankness can be traced through the pornography industry, which expanded rapidly during the 1970s as censorship standards relaxed… " (p. 32)

It does not take a rocket scientist to figure out that there is a lot of sexually charged stimulus in our culture. And this reality provides some major challenges for those of us who want to be "pure in heart" (Matthew 5: 8, NIV), faithful in our marriages, and examples of purity to others.

This is not just a male issue either. Some researchers have suggested that as many as 30% of the folks regularly viewing pornography today are female. And the number of women involved in Internet affairs and adulterous relationships indicates that this is a human problem.

Before we go any farther in our discussion of sexual immorality, let's take a look at the life of Samson, the Old Testament Judge, who was taken out because of immorality.

Samson

Samson was the son of Manoah from the clan of the Danites (Judges 13: 2). His mother was sterile (Judges 13:2) so his conception was miraculous. His birth was disclosed by an angel of the Lord who appeared to Manoah's wife (Judges 13: 3) and declared that Samson would be a Nazarite from birth and deliver Israel out of the hands of the Philistines (Judges 13: 5).

After Manoah's wife shared this with her husband he prayed to God for revelation on how to raise this son (Judges 13: 8). Again, the angel of the Lord appeared and instructed them both (Judges 13: 13-14). Manoah then made a sacrifice to God and the angel ascended in the flame (Judges 13: 19-20). The fear of God fell on Manoah from this encounter (Judges 13: 22) and shortly after this his wife gave birth to Samson (Judges 13: 24).

Samson grew up in what by all means would be considered a Godly home and "he grew and the Lord blessed him, and the Spirit of the Lord began to stir him…" (Judges 13: 24-25, NIV). Great start, but look what happens next – the teenage years! The Bible does not give us a lot of details, but as Samson becomes a young man he begins to notice the opposite sex (Judges 14: 1). Noticing the opposite sex is pretty natural, but read on in this passage.

Notice what happens next. Samson is attracted to a Philistine woman and he decides to marry her (Judges 14: 2). His father tries to talk him out of it, but he is sure that she is "the right one for me" (Judges 14: 3). Although the following passage says that "this was from the Lord" (Judges 14: 4), I suspect that this is one of those difficult passages where God uses someone in spite of compromise. I say this because in Deuteronomy 7: 3, the Bible states, "Do not intermarry with them… for they will turn your sons away from me to serve other gods…"

Let's see what happens next to Samson. He persuades his father and mother to accompany him to Timnah to marry the Philistine woman (Judges 14: 5). Along the way, Samson encounters a lion and (being empowered by the Spirit) kills it with his bare hands

(Judges 14: 6). He evidently was separated from his parents at this time as the Bible states that, "he told neither his father or mother what he had done" (Judges 14: 6). Again, a small detail has significant implications for Samson.

In Numbers 6, the Bible describes the "vow of separation to the Lord as a Nazarite." This vow involved three qualifications:

1. Abstinence from fermented drinks;
2. Letting his hair grow long; and
3. Staying away from dead bodies.

O.K., what happens next to Samson? Later, he visits the Philistine woman again "and turned aside to look at the lion's carcass" (Judges 14: 8a). He was probably far enough away from the carcass to meet the minimum requirements of his Nazarite vow, but there was a sweet treat ("honey") in the carcass that he just had to have (Judges 14: 8b). He scoops it out, ate it, and even shared it with his parents (Judges 14: 9a). No big deal, right? But why does the passage again include, "he did not tell them…" (Judges 14: 9b)?

Do you see what is happening here? I have learned in my own life and from studying the lives of others that it is the "small" stuff that ends up killing us! The reason why is that the small stuff is easier to rationalize which "covers up" for a while the reality that small stuff become big stuff if we do not repent and win the battle of the flesh.

I will not go into the soap opera affairs of the next several verses, but Samson's life was characterized by powerful demonstrations of the Spirit in vengeance on the Philistines and growing compromise in his moral life. Fast forward to Judges 16 and we read:

> "One day Samson went to Gaza, where he saw a prostitute. He went in to spend the night with her…" (verse 1) Some time later, he fell in love with a woman in the Valley of Sorek whose name was Delilah…" (verse 4, NIV)

Moral Barriers

It took some time, but finally Delilah, a spy for the Philistines (Judges 16: 5), was able to "nag" Samson into revealing the source of his great strength (Judges 16: 16-18). Delilah told the Philistines who cut off Samson's hair and "his strength left him" (Judges 16: 19).

Note what happens next. Samson thinks the power resides in him (remember that, "pride goes before destruction, a haughty spirit before a fall." Proverbs 16: 18, NIV). He thinks that he can get out of this situation just like he has gotten out of other ones. But something is different this time! Samson, "awoke from his sleep and thought, 'I'll go out as before and shake myself free.' But he did not know that the Lord had left him." (Judges 16: 20b)

Wow! What a train wreck!!!! And it does not get better. The next scene shows Samson chained with bronze shackles to a grinding wheel in prison (Judges 16: 21b). Not only this, but the Philistines "gauged out his eyes" (Judges 16: 21 a). Do you see the connection here? What a tragic picture of what unrestrained sin can lead to! Here, a once powerful man of God is enslaved, sightless, and walking in circles. Why? Because of his pride and his failure to deal with the "lust of the eyes" (I John 2: 16, NIV).

The story does not end here. Samson's hair grew back and he has one last victory when he collapses the pillars of the temple of Dagon on the Philistines. He "killed many more when he died than while he lived" (Judges 16: 30). Great victory – I do not think so!

I have found only two people in the Bible who died with their arms outstretched: Samson and Jesus. An examination of their last words is revealing. Samson prayed to God for strength to "get revenge on the Philistines for my two eyes" (Judges 16: 28). Jesus said while dying on the cross in the Luke account, "Father forgive them, for they do not know what they are doing" (Luke 23: 34, NIV). What a contrast: one wants revenge and the other one wants forgiveness!

Samson's life and legacy is one of great power and tragedy. He had so much potential, but because he failed to learn how to handle his sexuality in a Godly manner he finished badly and is remembered for all time for his immorality, not his spirituality.

What can we learn from the failure of Samson? A lot, I hope:

1. Even if we grow up in a godly home, we have to make our own decisions as an adult.
2. The decisions we make have long-term consequences.
3. If we allow sin to go unrepented, it will grow in its destructive power and may eventually control us and define our legacy.
4. We need to be teachable and accountable in areas where we are vulnerable to sin.
5. We need to cultivate humility to counteract our tendency to be arrogant.
6. We need to learn to forgive others (and ourselves).
7. We need to ultimately become more loving, kind, and merciful.

For our purposes here, I want to describe and illustrate the destructive nature of sexual immorality in the life and leadership of those who fail to establish the deep work of God's grace to purify our hearts (I Timothy 1: 5). We can learn from the tragic life of Samson and learn to deal with this powerful aspect of our humanity. If we do not, we can become entrapped by our sexuality.

Characteristics of Sexual addiction

Fred Stoeker and Steve Arteburn, in *Every Man's Battle*, list the following characteristics of addictive sexual behavior (p. 29):

1. Addictive sex is done in isolation.
2. Addictive sex is secretive.

Moral Barriers

3. Addictive sex is self-focused.
4. Addictive sex is victimizing.
5. Addictive sex ends in despair.
6. Addictive sex is used to escape pain and problems.

The usual point of access comes from exposure to various forms of pornography. If we do not learn to gain heart victory in the area of our sexuality, we can become vulnerable to addiction resulting in horrible consequences. Charles Stanley, in *Landmines*, list the following consequences of sexual sin (p. 200-204):

1. Guilt,
2. Self-condemnation,
3. Anxiety,
4. Divided mind,
5. Damaged self-esteem,
6. Feeling of hypocrisy,
7. Deep sense of emptiness,
8. Disappointment and lack of contentment,
9. Feeling of dishonesty,
10. Willful disobedience
11. Unspeakable regret,
12. Doubt,
13. Lack of effectiveness and wasted time,
14. Fear,
15. Broken relationships,
16. Damaged testimony,

17. Sexual addiction.

The momentary pleasure of sexual immorality is not worth going through this. There is a better way. It is possible to deal with our sexuality in pure and God honoring ways. And, if we do not, we will not finish well and some day will have to look back on our lives with regret. We do not want to end up like Samson!

2. Misuse of Finances

Those of us who live and lead in a Western context have it pretty well off materially. Most of us do not have to worry about survival needs on a daily basis as many do in the developing world. All it takes is one short-term outreach or business trip to the developing world (and getting out of a Western hotel to see the poverty of most people) to show the contrast between the haves and have-nots in our world.

This is not meant to be the start of a guilt trip for living in a wealthier context than most, but it is an attempt to be realistic so that we can be honest about material things and materialism. I like the way Richard Foster, in *Freedom of Simplicity*, frames this issue:

> "Few of us would buy into the naïve notion that the accumulation of bigger and better things will give us joy or purpose. Yet neither are we comfortable with the rigid ascetic who thunders down denunciations on the evil of possessions. We don't want to be materialists, ever acquiring and ever hoarding. And yet, John the Baptist with his skins and wild honey doesn't quite seem the model either. How can we put material things in a proper perspective in a world of dental bills and piano lessons? How do we decide for or against a new microwave oven or dishwasher?" (p. 15)

Money and possessions are not the ultimate issue. Materialism or the idolatry of economic security and fulfillment goes deeper that the stuff we have or the clothes we wear. The Bible warns:

> "Do not store up for yourselves treasures on earth, where moth and rust destroy, and where thieves break in and steal. But store up for yourselves treasures in heaven, where moth and rust do not destroy, and where thieves do not break in and steal. **For where your treasure is, there your heart will be also.**" (Matthew6: 16-21, NIV, **bold** added)

Jesus contrasts two types of treasures here: one earthly and one heavenly. I view the earthly treasure as materialism, which is temporal, and the heavenly treasures as godly and eternal. This does not mean that Jesus is teaching a strict type of asceticism, but he is pointing out that materialism can be a problem, a sort of idol, if we are not careful.

Other Biblical teachings on possessions include:

- Tithing
- Offerings
- Contentment
- Stewardship
- Generosity
- Service
- Sacrifice

As revealed in Jesus' teaching on earthly and heavenly treasures, the heart is the issue: "where [our] treasure is, there [our] heart will be also" (Matthew 7: 21, NIV). Let's now take a look at a Biblical leader who failed to finish well in life and leadership because of his misuse of finances.

Judas

Judas, surnamed Iscariot, was one of the twelve disciples that Jesus called to be with him (Matthew 10: 4, Mark 3: 19, 14: 10 and 43, Luke 6: 15, 22: 47, and John 6: 71). Although there are only about 24 passages in the New Testament that mention Judas by name, there is ample information about him to give us insights into what led ultimately to his betrayal of Jesus.

Judas was a secondary member of the twelve, with John, James, and Peter part of Jesus' inner circle (Matthew 17: 1, Mark 9: 2, Luke 9: 28). The fact that there seemed to be favorites amongst Jesus' disciples could have contributed to Judas' disillusionment with Jesus. We do not know for sure, but something happened along the way that ultimately led to betrayal.

We do know that Judas was the treasurer for Jesus' band of twelve disciples (John 13: 29) and that he would keep some of the money for himself (John 12: 6). This is very revealing, because it shows how patterns of sin lead to a double life (or hypocrisy) in Christian leaders. John described a situation in which a woman poured an expensive perfume on Jesus' feet to show her appreciation for his kindness to her. Look at Judas' response:

> "But one of his disciples, Judas Iscariot, who was later to betray him, objected, 'Why wasn't this perfume sold and the money given to the poor? It was worth a year's wages.' He did **not say this because he cared about the poor but because he was a thief**; as keeper of the money bag, he used to help himself to what was put into it." (John 12: 4-6, NIV, **bold** added)

Moral Barriers

A thief? That is pretty harsh! I am sure that Judas did not intend to be described as a thief (or even worse, the betrayer), but that is the nature of sin. He probably started "small." He probably was going to pay it back at first, but one thing led to another. Before long he was in deep and his sin (double life and hypocrisy) began to affect the way he related to Jesus and the others. Guilt, rationalization, and defense mechanisms led to distortion and defensiveness.

Unless we confront our sin, confess it (I John 1: 9), and repent (Matthew 4: 17), we become vulnerable to the digression of sin into wrath (see Romans 1: 18-32). We may think we can contain our sin, but we are mistaken. Sin is like cancer – it continues to grow and destroy unless it is removed or killed off.

And that is what happened in the life of Judas. There is no indication is the Biblical record that he conspired from the start to betray Jesus. In all likelihood, he got in over his head and one thing led to another. Before long, he probably found himself alienated from Jesus and the others, and open to the unimaginable: the betrayal of Jesus for 30 silver coins (Matthew 26: 15).

How did he get into this mess? The Bible sheds some light on it. After a sequence of events that included Jesus raising Lazarus from the dead (Luke 16 and John 11-12), the triumphal entry (Mark 11, Luke 19, and John 12), and the cleansing of the Temple (Mark 11 and Luke 19), the chief priests and teachers of the law had had enough:

> "Each day Jesus was teaching at the temple, and each evening he went out to spend the night on the hill called the Mount of Olives, and all the people came early in the morning to hear him at the temple. Now the Feast of the Unleavened Bread, called the Passover, was approaching, and the chief priests and teachers of the law were looking for some way to get rid of Jesus, for they were afraid of the people." (Luke 21: 37-22:2, NIV)

It is at this moment that Judas is vulnerable and Satan acts – a really bad combination! The Bible next reveals:

> "Then Satan entered Judas, called Iscariot, one of the Twelve. And Judas went to the chief priests and officers of the temple guard and discussed with them how he might betray Jesus. They were delighted and agreed to give him money. He consented, and watched for an opportunity to hand Jesus over to them when no crowd was present." (Luke 22: 3-6, NIV)

Nasty sequence here which only gets worse with Judas ultimately betraying Jesus on the Mount of Olives with a kiss (Luke 22: 47-48). What happened next is recorded in great detail in the four Gospels: arrest, trial, crucifixion, resurrection, ascension, and the promise of the second coming. For Judas, his life spins totally out of control. Who knows what he was thinking while planning and implementing his betrayal of Jesus, but his end was tragic:

> "When Judas, who had betrayed him, saw that Jesus was condemned, he was seized with remorse and returned the thirty silver coins to the chief priests and elders. 'I have sinned,' he said, 'for I have betrayed innocent blood.'" (Matthew 27: 3-4, NIV)

What a sad ending to a life that seemed to have so much potential. He was chosen as one of the twelve, traveled with Jesus through towns and villages as he ministered (Matthew 9: 35), participated in powerful short-term outreaches (Matthew 10), was entrusted with the finances of the team, witnessed miracles (John 21: 25), etc. All this and in the end the most often used phrase in the Bible to describe Judas is the "betrayer" or "the one who betrayed him."

Out of despair Judas took his own life and even the money that he returned to the chief priests and elders was viewed as "blood money" and used to purchase a field "as a burial place for foreigners" called "the Field of Blood" (Matthew 27: 5-8, NIV).

Moral Barriers

I understand that there are a lot of complex issues involved in examining the life of Judas, but what I am interested in is what I can learn from his tragic story. Here are a few insights that have helped me and I hope will help you:

1. We are all like Judas, in that we are fallen human beings, who have the capacity of sin.

2. We have the capacity to rationalize sinful attitudes and actions.

3. We have the capacity to use defense mechanisms to make ourselves look better than we really are.

4. Sin cannot be contained. We have to either deal with it through confession and repentance or it will continue to grow and cause unthinkable consequences.

5. As a Christian leader, we need to live "above reproach" (I Timothy 3: 2) in our inner and outer lives.

6. As a Christian leader, we need to be open and submitted to honest and healthy accountability.

I want someone counting the offering with me! I want someone looking over my shoulder when it comes to my budget (income and expenditures). I want to make sure that I am tithing, that I am generous, and a good steward of the possessions that God has given me. Although, having money is not the ultimate issue, it may well be part of the circumstances that lead us into a place of vulnerability. The Bible warns:

> "People who want to get rich fall into temptation and a trap and into many foolish and harmful desires that plunge men [and women] into ruin and destruction. For the love of money is a root of all kinds of evil. Some people, eager for money, have wandered from the faith and pierced themselves with many griefs." (I Timothy 6: 9-10, NIV)

3. Misuse of Authority

There are three primary "bases" of authority (personal, positional, and spiritual) that express themselves in four "power forms" (J. Robert Clinton, *Clinton's Biblical Leadership Commentary*, p. 439). These power forms are:

- **Force** – the use of physical or psychic influence to gain compliance.

- **Manipulation** – compliance of followers where the follower does not have awareness of a leader's intents and therefore, does not necessarily have freedom to exert moral responsibility in his/her decision making.

- **Persuasion** – the use of argument, appeal, and exhortation to gain compliance.

- **Authority** – the use of promises of reward to gain compliance.

All four power forms, for good or bad, are probably at play in most leader-follower influence exchanges, but spiritual authority is the primary base and form for those who finish well in life and leadership. Clinton defines spiritual authority as, "the right to influence conferred upon a leader by followers because of their perception of spirituality in that leader" (p. 441). Leaders who function in spiritual authority influence their followers through:

- Godliness

- Modeling

- Persuasion

Moral Barriers

This type of authority comes from life transformation forged through the pressure of life situations (James 1: 2-4), through maturity of character (Galatians 5: 22-26), and spiritual gifts (Romans 12, I Corinthians 12, Ephesians 4) exercised in love (I Corinthians 13). Clinton, in *The Making of a Leader*, describes 10 qualities of spiritual authority that he calls "Ten Commandments of Spiritual Authority" (p. 102):

1. One who learns spiritual authority as the power base for ministry [leadership] must recognize the essential Source of all authority: God.

2. God's delegated authority does not belong to the person exercising it – that person is just a channel.

3. The channel of delegated authority is responsible to God for how that authority is exercised.

4. A leader is one who recognizes God's authority manifested in real-life situations.

5. Subjection to authority means that a person is subject to God himself and not to the channel through which the authority comes.

6. Rebellion against authority means that a person is not subjecting himself to God, though it may appear that the person is rejecting some impure manifestation of God's authority through a human channel.

7. People who are under God's authority look for and recognize spiritual authority and willingly place themselves under it.

8. Spiritual authority is never exercised for one's own benefit, but for those under it.

9. A person in spiritual authority does not have to insist on obedience – that is the moral responsibility of the follower.

10. God is responsible to defend spiritual authority.

This does not mean that there will never be disagreements and conflicts between leaders who are functioning in spiritual authority. Loving disagreement can lead to creative options and solutions. And some disagreements may result in new kingdom ventures (as with Paul and Barnabas in Acts 15: 36-41). When such disagreements occur, we need to love one another (John 13: 34) and be at peace with others "as far as it depends on you" (Romans 12: 18, NIV).

Unfortunately, the misuse of power and authority is way too common in both the marketplace and in ministry. No leader is perfect except Jesus and even he had some challenges in his leadership. My sense is that way too many Christians in leadership roles are relying on personal and positional authority without cultivating a balance of spiritual authority. The results are futile at best and tragic in way too many instances. Ken Blue, in his book *Healing Spiritual Abuse*, is helpful here. He describes the primary characteristics of what he calls "spiritual abusers" (p. 134-135) from his study of the Pharisees in Matthew 23:

1. Abusive leaders base their spiritual authority on their position or office rather than their service to the group. Their style of leadership is authoritarian.

2. Leaders in abusive churches [organizations] often say one thing but do another. Their words and deeds do not match.

3. They manipulate people by making them feel guilty for not measuring up spiritually. They lay heavy religious loads on people and make no effort to lift those loads…

4. Abusive leaders are preoccupied with looking good. They labor to keep up appearance. They stifle any criticism that puts them in a bad light.

5. They seek honorific titles and special privileges that elevate them above the group. They promote a class system with themselves at the top.

6. Their communication is not straight. Their speech becomes especially vague and confusing when they are defending themselves.

7. They major on minor issues to the neglect of the truly important ones. They are conscientious about religious details but neglect God's larger agendas.

With this contrast between spiritual authority and spiritual abuse in mind, let's take a look at the life of Saul as a tragic example of someone who failed to finish well because of his failure to deal with issues in his life leading to a reliance on personal and positional authority rather than spiritual authority.

Saul

Saul was the son Kish, a Benjamite, and is described as "an impressive young man without equal among the Israelites – a head taller than any of the others" (I Samuel 9: 1-2, NIV). While on a journey to find some lost donkeys he came into contact with the prophet ("seer") Samuel (I Samuel 9: 14) who had heard already from God that they would meet (I Samuel 9: 15-16a) and that Saul was to be "anointed" leader over Israel (I Samuel 9: 16b). Saul is on the fast track. He has the right stuff, right? Not only is he the best of the best, but also Samuel promises him that:

"The Spirit of the Lord will come upon you in power, and you will prophecy... and you will be changed into a different person. Once these signs are fulfilled, do whatever your hands find to do, for God is with you." (I Samuel 10: 6-7, NIV)

All of this came to pass (I Samuel 10: 9-11) and Saul becomes the first king of Israel (I Samuel 10: 20-25). What a success story! Or was it? A closer reading of the text reveals some interesting information and insights into Saul. First, the whole king idea was not what God intended for his people (I Samuel 10: 19). The problem with kings is that they are human, with all their potential and sinfulness. As we see from the Old Testament accounts of the kings there were some (very few) good ones and many bad ones.

Second, Saul, in spite of his recent encounter with the Spirit of the Lord, became overwhelmingly aware of his humanity - probably he became self-conscious or felt inadequate. When the people ask Samuel where their new king was, they find him "hid[ing] himself among the baggage" (I Samuel 10: 22b). The people had to bring him out of hiding, but because of his stature (I Samuel 10: 23), they get all excited and proclaim, "Long live the king!" (I Samuel 10: 24).

Third, as king, Saul had to face the challenging realities of working with people, some of whom did not like him (I Samuel 10: 26-27). Note that, "They despised him and brought him no gifts" (verse 27). Leadership can be challenging and hurtful. Not everyone is going to agree with us or like us!

Shortly after this Saul led the Israelites into battle with the Ammonites (I Samuel 11). The Spirit of God came upon Saul in power (I Samuel 11: 6) and he led 330,000 men ("as one man") from Israel and Judah to victory against the Ammonites (I Samuel 11: 7b-11). There is a little intrigue that I left out, but Saul is off to a pretty good start as king. The people are happy with his leadership and celebrated his great victory and reaffirmed his kingship (I Samuel 11: 14-15).

Moral Barriers

At this point in the story, Samuel went into semi-retirement after giving the people a farewell message (I Samuel 12). He said something interesting in this message that gives important insights into the importance of leadership in the unfolding of God's redemptive story. He warned the people:

> "Now here is the king you have chosen, the one you ask for; see, the Lord has set a king over you. If you fear the Lord and serve and obey him and do not rebel against his commands, and if both you and the king who reigns over you follow the Lord your God – good! But if you do not obey the Lord, and if you rebel against his commandments, his hand will be against you, as it was against your fathers." (I Samuel 12: 13-15, NIV)

O.K. Let's see how this story worked out. God showed up again in power, this time through thunder and rain and the people come under the "awe of the Lord" and repented for choosing a king (I Samuel 12: 18-19). Samuel responded by reminding them that God had chosen them and would not reject them (I Samuel 12: 22), although their heart obedience would determine the quality of their lives (see I Samuel 12: 20 and 24-25).

The next sequence of our story finds Saul leading Israel into battle against the superior forces of the Philistines (I Samuel 13: 5). Outmatched, Saul and his men waited in fear for Samuel at Gilgal (I Samuel 13: 7b). After seven days, when Samuel failed to show, Saul decided to conduct burnt and fellowship offerings to calm his troops who were beginning to dissert (I Samuel 13: 8-9). Just as Saul finished making the offerings, Samuel showed up and rebuked Saul for assuming the role of priest (I Samuel 13: 10-14).

Of course, Saul had his reasons for what he did. They sounded pretty good under the circumstances. But the problem is that Saul knew better (see I Samuel 10: 25) and was not obedient. Big mistake! Samuel rebuked him and shared with him that there would be dire consequences because of his disobedience (I Samuel 13: 13-14). It is pretty much down hill from here:

- Israel came under the oppression of the Philistines and their army lost their weapons (I Samuel 13).

- Throughout the rest of Saul's reign there was "bitter war with the Philistines" (I Samuel 14: 52).

- Saul allowed his troops to keep "the best sheep and cattle to sacrifice" in disobedience and Samuel confronted Saul again (I Samuel 15) with the words, "To obey is better than sacrifice... rebellion is like the sin of divination, and arrogance like the evil of idolatry" (verses 22b and 23).

With this act of disobedience, Saul was rejected as king (I Samuel 15: 23b). At this point, an interesting exchange occurs between Saul and Samuel (I Samuel 15: 24-31). Saul said all the right words of repentance, but the core of his heart is also revealed. Note, that Saul said, "I was afraid of the people and so I gave into them" (verse 24) and later, "Please honor me before the elders... and before Israel" (verse 30). Saul was more concerned about looking good to the people than he was about being obedient to God. Saul never dealt with this need for approval from man and ultimately it turned him into a bitter man and an inept leader who abused others and led the nation into disaster!

What a sad story! But we can learn from Saul's life so that we do not end up bitter abusers of our power base and authority. As I look at the life of Saul I am reminded of several important lessons:

1. We all want to be liked by and look good to others, but obedience is more important than being liked or looking good.

2. Spiritual authority is primarily a matter of the heart and must be cultivated through obedience.

Moral Barriers

3. Being a "man pleaser" opens us up to comparison, jealousy, and bitterness.

4. The purpose of personal and positional authority is to honor God and serve others (not to manipulate or force our agenda on others).

5. Over the long haul we must learn how to balance personal and positional authority with spiritual authority as our core power base for influence.

6. We all have the capacity to be pragmatic (especially when under pressure), but in the kingdom the end never justifies fleshly means.

7. Humility, being teachable, and accountability are safeguards for pride, isolation, and self-serving.

The tragic lives of these three Bible leaders ought to be a wake-up call for us. All three of these guys were heavy weights. They seemed to have everything going for them: good looks, athletic accomplishment, education, contacts, success, etc. But they did not develop the moral character necessary to finish well. All three left legacies of compromise, failure, and hurt.

Certainly moral character and integrity are critical issues that we must address if we intend to finish well, but they are not the only issues that we will face. In the next chapter, Richard will lead us through three relational barriers (pride, marriage and family, and emotional wounding) that have also caused far too many leaders to stumble before reaching the finish line.

Application and Discussion Questions:

1. What did your learn about moral barriers to finishing well by reading this chapter?

2. What insights have you gained from the case studies on those who failed to finish well because of sexual immorality, misuse of finances, or misuse of authority?

3. What additional insights (apart from the reading) have you gained as you have reflected on the content of this chapter?

4. As a man/woman, which of these three barriers do you think your gender struggles with most? Why?

5. Which of these barriers do you struggle with? Why do you think you struggle with it and what have you learned that has helped you gain victory in this struggle?

6. Do you have an accountability partner who you can go to for support, encouragement, and honest evaluation? If so, how has that been helpful? If not, why (and what are you waiting for)?

Chapter 4

Relational Barriers

Many years ago, I (Richard) heard one of my professors say the following, "Psychologists tell us that when we get older we don't get better we just become more of who we really are." I did not write down who said that, but I have remembered the quote ever sense. There is something about the aging process that breaks down our inhibitions. Maybe in younger years we are more concerned about what people think and we try to reveal to people only what we want them to see. As we get older, we do not seem to be as interested in playing these kinds of image games. As the famous comedian Flip Wilson used to say, "what you see is what you get."

I believe that this is especially true when it comes to our relationships as we grow older. Who we really are is not easy to hide in the context of our close relationships. Three of the major barriers to finishing well deal directly with relationships. Each barrier can creep into a leader's life in different ways. We must take precautions against issues that can derail us as we move towards finishing well.

Three Relational Barriers in the End Game

One of the barriers deals with our *marriages and families*. Who we are is clear to the members of our families and those who are closest to us. It is the people closest to us that see most clearly the differences between the leader out there and the leader at home. This barrier represents one of the biggest challenges for leaders during the end game.

Another barrier to finishing well that affects our relationships *is wrongful pride*. Wrongful pride surfaces in our relationships with the people that we work with. It also surfaces in our relationship to God and the ministry that we do. In the end game, leaders are operating at the peak of their ministry effectiveness and there are temptations to make some poor decisions and deflect some of God's glory onto us. Or there can be temptations to take God's role and make things happen. We have to avoid these temptations.

A third major barrier that affects our relationships is the barrier that we have called *emotional wounding*. Over a lifetime of ministry involvement, we all experience relational challenges that emerge when we interact with people. A recent leadership survey revealed that 80% of pastors report that they go through at least one major conflict with another person every month. Working in the Kingdom of God means that we are working with people. Working with people means going through countless misunderstandings, conflicts, personality conflicts, and a hundred other kinds of relational experiences.

How a leader handles these encounters makes a huge difference in the kind of wounding that they carry forward in ministry. If not handled well, our lack of healing will cause us to react to others out of our wounding. Reacting and leading out of a place of wounding can derail us as we try to finish well.

1. Marriage and Family Issues in the End Game

Another one of the huge barriers that can prevent leaders from finishing well is their family and all the relationships that are represented. Because we have dealt with the importance of marriage in the second book of this series, I won't go into great detail here.

There are several issues that leaders in the end game deal with that are unique. Throughout human history, no matter how family is defined, this network of relationships is complicated. The dynamics of these relationships can cause layers of problems that have to be navigated throughout life and especially in the end game. Many leaders fail to finish well because they get mired in family situations that hinder them from doing what God designed them to do.

By the time we get to the end game, family issues that most leaders are dealing with are complex issues that are further complicated by issues related to aging. There are health issues that come into play. There can be limitations put on leaders because of health concerns that force changes. What is possible to do or not possible can change with a single medical report or illness. Many leaders have to deal with the death of a spouse and all of the complexity that comes with that. These are significant issues that need to be navigated in the end game if one wants to finish well.

A leader who finished well that I greatly respect was my grandmother Clinton. She was a spiritual powerhouse in our family. From the perspective of a grandchild, I observed her steadfastness and her consistency in dealing with many setbacks in life. When I was a young pastor in my 20's, I began to see her as not only my grandmother, but also as a spiritual leader. Her entire life she ministered bi-vocationally. I don't know how many people she influenced through her lifetime. She held a number of different jobs. I only knew her as a nursing home administrator. The nursing home where she worked supported our family when we were missionaries so we would go visit them when we were there. In the last 15-20 years of her life, she faced a number of incredibly painful and difficult situations. My grandfather died. My grandmother was diagnosed with several life threatening and painful diseases that she had to battle. In all of those things, her character stayed the same. Her commitment to God never wavered. Her passion for God's word stayed steadfast.

The people close to her shared at her funeral that she was one of the most courageous women and leaders that they had ever seen. Her end game was not easy by any measurement, but she made it through to the celebration that was waiting for her. I find myself wondering how she found the strength to do what she did. My dad says, "She cultivated her character through a lifetime of choices (mostly unseen). She dedicated herself to truth and learning the truth. And she loved God and people." My father has picked up many of those values and lives them out as well. I am working to do the same.

In addition to this, if we are married with children, the children are grown and producing grandchildren. How we deal with all of the issues that they are facing affects our end game. In our own family, I have watched my parents, who are leaders in their end game, try to cope with, help out and try to figure out what to do as each one of my sisters and my brother and I make our way through life. Their generation coped with life's circumstances differently and the cultural values that they grew up with have shifted. My parents are not wired to deal with the complexities of what is going on with my siblings and me. This has added a great deal of stress and pressure to their end game. I think the same will be true of me as I process what is going on with my own kids and their families.

There are financial issues and many times these financial difficulties cause major pressure. In the group of churches where I work, we don't have a financial system of caring for our pastors as they move towards retirement. Our group of churches is under 30 years old. I know of many pastors who are moving into their end game and facing some challenging financial realities. The financial pressure for many leaders means trying to work well into the 70's. This greatly changes what the end game looks like.

There are not a lot of family or marriage stories in the Bible that we can relate to. Many of the Old Testament stories involve cultural settings and practices that we cannot relate to. King David had one of the most complicated and difficult family situations imaginable. He had multiple wives, a favorite wife, an attempted coup by his son Absalom and other sons who were fighting for power. What a mess! Most of us cannot relate to something like this in our cultural setting.

We are fortunate today that we have a lot of resources to help us keep our marriage relationships healthy and vital. There are scores of competent people and excellent materials that can help us navigate the complexities of family systems as we move through the different seasons of life. Financial planners can help us prepare for the realities of the end game by helping us make the informed decisions about retirement income.

I want to make one last comment when it comes to leaders facing family issues in the end game. One of the most beneficial things that we can do is pass on the values that have shaped our lives. This is especially true if we have kids and grand kids. I first noticed family values in my grandparents. It made me want to ask my parents questions. What I wanted was to hear about the stories that shaped their lives and that have shaped my parents lives and then influenced my own life.

Storytelling, which captures values, is important. Taking the time to capture critical incidents in the formation of a family is important. Finding a way to demonstrate values is worth the effort. This is especially true in the relationship between grandparents and grandchildren. It is not always possible, but whenever possible, we should take advantage of it. Connecting values to life decisions is one of the most valuable things that we can pass on. It is a major part of the heritage and legacy that we leave behind.

2. The Barrier of Wrongful Pride in the End Game

Let me share a couple of Biblical examples of how wrongful pride ruins leaders and keeps them from finishing well. First, lets take a look at the life of King Asa.

King Asa

In 1 Kings 15 and 2 Chronicles 14-16, we are told the story of King Asa. King Asa was considered one of the kings that did what was pleasing and good in the sight of God. He ruled in Judah for 41 years. His reign was one of the longest in the southern kingdom. We are told that in his early years there was peace in Judah and he instituted many God honoring reforms. Then came the threat of war from a huge army advancing from Ethiopia. We are told that Asa turned to God and put his trust in him. God defeated the Ethiopians and gave Asa a great victory. After the battle, he received a prophecy that he had honored God and that God would honor him as long as he stayed faithful to God.

From that time until his 35th year as king, the people of Judah experienced peace. But tensions began to grow with the northern kingdom led by King Baasha. In the 36th year of Asa's reign, King Baasha invaded northern Judah and captured Ramah. After 36 years of being faithful to God, King Asa made a decision to hire King Ben-hadad, the king of Aram to come and fight against King Baasha. We are not told why King Asa made this decision. The implication in the text is that he took matters into his own hands and tried to solve the problem with the resources that he had. This was a prideful act. Maybe 35 years of a successful reign had affected King Asa. In the beginning, maybe he knew that he was dependent on God and threw his trust on Yahweh. After a long time of peace and success, King Asa began to see himself as not needing God as before. We really don't know.

Relational Barriers

God sends Hanani, a seer, to King Asa to point out the problem of King Asa's decision to put his trust in the King of Aram rather than put his trust in God. It is in this context that we have this great verse: "For the eyes of the LORD range throughout the earth to strengthen those whose hearts are fully committed to him" (2 Chronicles 16: 9). Then Hanani, the seer, tells King Asa what the consequences of his decision would bring on him and the people of Judah. God directs Hanani to say, "You have done a foolish thing, and from now on you will be at war" (2 Chronicles 16: 9). What a terrible decision! What had been a long and God honoring kingship comes crashing down because of wrongful pride.

What is especially revealing is how King Asa responded to the prophet and how he responded to the people that he was leading. The text says, "Asa was angry with the seer because of this; he was so enraged that he put him in prison. At the same time Asa brutally oppressed some of the people" (2 Chronicles 16: 10). What a tragedy! What makes a leader who was loved by the people, honored and protected by God turn in this direction? Wrongful pride!

King Asa turns against the prophet and the people because he does not want to own his mistake. He does not want to accept that what was happening was a result of his own actions. Instead, he reacts with anger and turns that anger outward against the people around him. This is what happens when wrongful pride gains control.

King Asa started well. King Asa enjoyed favor in the middle game and continued well. But at the end, it all came crashing down. This example is a strong warning for all of us who are in the end game. One of the dangers of a long successful ministry filled with favor from God and people is that we can allow that to become a seedbed for pride. If we do not continue to recognize that all the glory and honor belong to God, we can become prideful and fall. If we do not take steps to recognize God's part and to stay in a posture of humility regarding our part, we can fall.

In the last two years of King Asa's reign, we are told that he became afflicted with a serious disease in his feet. Filled with bitterness, he turns to his own devices and physicians to find healing rather than to humble himself and turn back to God. This is the end result of a life that is sabotaged and derailed by wrongful pride.

King Uzziah

King Uzziah was a strong king in the southern kingdom of Judah. He began his reign when he was 16 years old. He reigned for 52 years. In 2 Chronicles 26, we are told of all the great things that he accomplished in his long and successful reign as king. He was mentored by Zechariah, who taught him to seek God in all things. King Uzziah learned to seek God and God gave him favor. He won battles against their long time enemies, the Philistines. He fortified and rebuilt the infrastructure of Judah and made it strong. His armies were organized well and ready to serve. His army was well supplied and trained and he even made advancements in strategy and defense around Jerusalem. His fame spread far and wide.

Then, we read one of those sad verses in the Bible - "but when he became powerful, he became proud, which led to his downfall" (2 Chronicles 26: 16). What did King Uzziah do? We are told that he entered the sanctuary of God's temple and went to burn incense before God. On the surface, this doesn't sound so bad. But Uzziah knew what he was doing was wrong. The high priest and eighty other priests confronted him. It was not his rightful role. King Uzziah had tried to bypass the authority that God had ordained by taking things into his own hands. What a mistake!

In response to the confrontation, King Uzziah turned and began 'raging' at the priests. As he did that, God struck him with leprosy that grew in front of their eyes. The priests rushed him out of the temple. I can only imagine the shock and terror that King Uzziah felt in that moment. The end result of this prideful act was that King Uzziah had to live in isolation and his kingdom was turned over to his son. What a tragic finish!

Most of us don't relate to the burning of incense or the temple worship so this story does not hit our hearts too strongly. But let me bring the story into clearer focus. What was Uzziah's sin? He has tried to bypass God's established authority and decided to do it 'his way'. How often are we tempted to bypass God and try to do things our 'own way'? This is the heart issue of wrongful pride!

In the end game, we should know who God is and what he has established. In my experience, the place where we are challenged the most in this issue is when we have to make decisions about how we are going to get a certain result. You see, King Uzziah was doing something good. Burning incense before the Lord was a way of worshipping and acknowledging Yahweh. But the means he employed was the problem.

To put it bluntly, does the end ever justify the means? As long as we end up with 'incense being burned before the Lord' does it matter how we get there? You bet it does! For God, both the means and the end are critical. As leaders we all know the temptation to cut corners or make decisions that are in the grey areas. We must avoid this temptation. It will lead us into wrongful pride and our leadership can come crashing down just like it did for King Uzziah.

Moses

Maybe one of the most difficult leadership stories for us to accept is the story of Moses and the rock. You know the story that I am referring to so let me jump ahead. Where does the end of Moses' story occur? Mt. Nebo in Moab. Really? Yes! But where should the story of Moses have ended? Somewhere in the Promised Land! Right?

Moses finished well, kind of. He is by far the most incredible leader that we have in the Old Testament. There are so many stories, so many challenges, so many things that Moses went through. I think that most of us as leaders read through the events of his life and leadership and marvel at all that God did through this man. God, himself, called Moses the most humble man on the face of the earth. We know how long it took God to work this humility into Moses. Moses walked closer to God than any other person except Jesus. And even with all that, his end was in Moab.

We all know the reason why. Moses was provoked as he responded to a bunch of grumpy, complaining people. The story is told in Numbers 20 - Moses struck the rock instead of speaking to it. In frustration, Moses yelled out, "Must we (speaking for his brother Aaron and himself) bring you water out of the rock?" (Verse10). Most messages have focused in on these two issues and pointed out that Moses sinned against God by not following God's directions exactly and more importantly, making it sound like he and Aaron were the ones bringing the water out of the rock. This 'act of pride' is what most interpreters point to when they speak of Moses' sin.

It is a difficult passage for all of us who have ever led grumpy, complaining people. Being provoked by followers can often lead us to respond out of emotion. It is in these situations that we must be extremely careful. I think that the warning of this text is a critical one. It is very important that we take extreme caution when we are doing ministry. We must not take any of the glory or honor that belongs to God for ourselves. We need to be careful not to exaggerate our actions and our part of what God is doing. For those of us who speak often and tell stories, this is especially true. We all know how easy it is to stretch the truth of a story to make ourselves sound a little better than we really were.

In the end game, we are operating in the most significant ministry roles that we will probably ever have. We will more than likely have the responsibility of making significant decisions about resources and people. We will have to respond to tense situations and circumstances that will test our faith. This is the nature of leadership. It is in these moments that we must exercise the caution that comes out of this story with Moses. His example was recorded for us so that we could learn from his mistake.

I once heard a message about humility. In the message there was a definition of humility that I have never forgotten. Before the definition of humility was given, two definitions of pride were given. Pride as we normally think about it is thinking too highly of ourselves. A second kind of pride is what was called false humility. This kind of pride is not thinking highly enough about yourself. It manifests itself in situations where people put themselves down or see themselves as less than they really are.

Then humility was defined like this: true humility is not thinking too highly of yourself and not thinking too little of yourself. True humility is thinking of yourself as God sees you. True humility is agreeing with what God says about you. These definitions have helped me by providing real guidelines to move forward in my leadership development. I want to be the best that I can be and push for everything that God has for me. But I do not want to go too far. I do not want to settle for too little either.

Some leaders (depending on their ego strength) will have the tendency of moving into pride while other will have the tendency of moving into false humility. To find the balance between the two means getting close enough to God to know exactly what God has designed and ordained for you. This is the key. Leaders who are finishing well have done this and continue to do it right up until the end.

3. Emotional Wounding in the End Game

This barrier is one that I first noticed when trying to help potential leaders get into the game. I kept noticing a hesitation or the tendency to step back right at the moment when they should have been stepping forward. There was something in them that was blocking them or hindering them from getting started.

Then I began working with a lot of leaders in the middle game. I noticed that there were a lot of leaders who just got stuck or blocked in their growth and development. They kept running into the same kind of problems with people over and over. I would see patterns of behavior in them and wonder what was causing that to come up in them.

Then I remembered a day when this issue became very personal to me. I was sitting in one of the most beautiful places in the world. I was at a retreat center in the Swiss Alps helping to lead a special training weekend for potential and emerging leaders. I was talking to the co-leader of the training and we were talking about our journeys. He then made a comment that I will never forget. The comment was made almost as a side comment. He said, "Richard, have you ever noticed that you have the tendency to put yourself down when you tell your story." He went on to say, "When you do it, it is kind of a humble way to speak and that is good, but I wonder if there is more going on." At that moment, it was like the air was sucked out of the room. I knew intuitively that he had touched on something that God was putting his finger on.

A little context is needed to fully understand. I had been really crying out to God in prayer about the ministry that I was involved in, wanting God to reveal what he was doing. The ministry was going pretty well. There were a lot of positives and I loved many things about it. At the same time, I had this gnawing feeling deep inside that I was somehow stuck and I was not moving forward. There were many external circumstances that I could point to which limited me, but what I really was wondering was, "Was there something inside of me that was blocking me? What is the problem?"

Then my friend made the comment mentioned above. I had noticed the 'tendency' to speak about the ministry and myself in the way that he was pointing out. But it seemed natural to me. We prayed together and in that moment the Holy Spirit helped me to understand what was really going on. This false humility was something that traced through my life and ministry for many years. In that prayer time (and many more sense), I asked God to expose the root of what was going on and bring healing. It would take too long to explain the whole healing process so I will summarize it for you here.

I went through some deep brokenness experiences in my 20's. During that time, I allowed some feelings and thoughts about myself to take root. These were contrary to what God really thought about me, but in trying to deal with the pain I bought into some of the lies that the enemy was speaking to me. These untruths came out in the way I perceived myself and they shaped my expectations about what could happen in and through me in my leadership. Sounds complicated? Not really. I had exchanged God's truth for something other than his truth. Twenty years later, I found myself blocked and stuck. And as I began to unravel this, I realized that if I didn't get this healed, I would be stuck in the phase of leadership development and I would be unable to step into anything else that God had for me.

Along the way I have been a part of helping many leaders get perspective on what God is doing in their lives. A lifetime of ministry is not easy. Because of the pressure and the people challenges, we will face a ton of situations where we may get wounded. How we move towards healing and gain perspective is crucial to moving out of the middle game into the end game.

Three Critical Emotional Issues

There are three critical emotional issues that I would like to point out that leaders have to deal with as they move through the middle game and into the end game. Different personalities will cope or manage these issues differently but I think we all have to face them one way or another.

The first emotional issue is *forgiveness*. This has been an issue for me at every stage of life and ministry. So much of our emotional wellbeing is connected to this issue. Have we learned how to forgive? Have we learned how to live out a lifestyle of forgiveness? By the end game, we all have learned the importance of this issue. We know that it is crucial in our relationship to God and with people. In the end game, we are thinking about consolidating what God has done in our lives. This throws us into thinking back on and reflecting about what has happened. This may bring up those incidents where our ability to forgive was tested. How did we do?

The second issue is dealing with the *sense of loss*. Depression is the normal reaction to loss. In the end game, there are a number of circumstances that emerge that contain a certain degree of loss. Moving into retirement contains a number of challenges or losses. On the one side, one looks forward to the changes and on the other side, one wonders what it will be like. There is an accompanying loss of identity that comes with a change in our leadership position. Dr. Archibald Hart has done some of the best work that I am aware of on outlining the issues that ministers or leaders face in the area of depression.

The third issue is the tendency, as we get older *to become more cynical or pessimistic*. I know that this is not true for everyone, but I know that it is true for many. Maybe it is because of all the stories that we could tell about the hardships and disappointments of ministry. I have heard the following on countless occasions - A younger leader sharing their new vision or direction, something they are going to launch or try in ministry. An older leader responding with, "Years ago, when I tried exactly what you are describing, we learned _____." There is wisdom that comes with experience, but there can also be a kind of pessimism as well.

Operating in faith seems to be more challenging the more one knows about what it takes for ministry efforts to succeed. Where this is especially dangerous is when we take this kind of tendency or attitude into our evaluations or estimations of people. We see things in younger leaders that could go well or badly. Which way will we choose to see it? I have been involved in my group of churches for nearly 30 years now. I have been a young leader in the movement and now I am one of the older leaders. I have seen leaders rise and fall. Not long ago, we were in another critical time of leadership transition so there was a lot of talk, evaluating, and speculating about what God was doing and what would happen. It was interesting to notice how I was responding. Which way would I lean? Would I respond with faith and optimism? Or would I respond with cynicism and pessimism? This is an issue that every leader has to face.

What's the antidote? Begin by recognizing that the tendency is there. Choose to guard your hearts against it. Stay soft hearted towards God. Remember how God looks at each one of us. His love for us causes him to choose to believe in us. This helps us in our view of people and the challenging situations that we face.

Conclusion

There is so much that could be said about these three barriers to finishing well. As we enter the end game, our foundations have already been laid. Out of those foundations, we respond to what the end game brings. Dealing with our marriage and family dynamics will stretch us in the end game. Fighting off the temptation to step into wrongful pride will take discipline. Continuing to pursue healing for our emotional wounds will take commitment. The good news is that leaders would not be in the end game if they had not done the hard work to establish good foundations. And they have a track record of experiencing God's faithfulness so they know that they can trust him.

Application and Discussion Questions:

1. How would you characterize your history of relationships throughout your ministry? Are there any tendencies or patterns that you identify that might cause problems in the end game?

2. If yes, what can you learn and what adjustments can be made to enhance the way you finish your race?

3. Are there any special issues relating to your marriage and family that need some special attention?

Starting Well

4. How have you had to battle against wrongful pride? What measures have you taken to guard against the danger that pride can cause?

5. What are the emotional issues that you face that you will have to navigate through? How are you coping with the issues that were raised?

Chapter 5

Faith Barriers

I (Paul) have seen so many good leaders loose their nerve and play it safe as they get closer to the end game of life and leadership. They once were innovators and risk takers, but over time they became more careful, even resistant to taking risks. They once were idealistic and now they are the status quo. This is called plateauing and is one of the two faith barriers that can keep leaders from finishing well and leaving a lasting legacy. In this chapter we will take a closer look at these two barriers:

1. *Plateauing* – Gideon (Judges 6-8)
2. *Boundaries* – Thomas (John 20-21)

What is Plateauing?

There are probably some pretty technical definitions for plateauing, but I like to think of it in terms of the "inability to continue following God in faithful and fruitful ways because of a lack of trust in God going forward." This definition suggests,

1. Inability – we lack resources necessary to face real life/ministry challenges.

2. Following God – our primary relationship and purpose in life.

3. Faithful – we need to cultivate the ability to hear God's voice and obey.

4. Fruitful – we are meant to reproduce "in kind" and leave a legacy for generations to come and for eternity.

BECAUSE OF:

5. Lack of Trust – lack of confidence in God and relational faithfulness to him resulting in Christ-like transformation in our attitudes and behavior toward others.

Plateauing can happen within the context of unresolved hurt and a sense of failure or ongoing success. Plateauing is subtler than most of the other barriers because there might not be the types of disastrous consequences that are associated with them.

The subtly of plateauing is that there is a connection between what is happening in leadership personally and organizationally. Leaders influence the cultures of the organizations that they lead. The research by Jim Collins, *How the Mighty Fall*, is very insightful here. In the past, many organizational experts believed that plateauing and decline occurred because of the impact of poor leadership and bureaucracy after the founding entrepreneurial leader transitions. What Collins discovered is that the DNA for plateauing and decline actually begins much earlier than previously thought. He states (p. 20-21):

> "Great enterprises can become insulated by successes; accumulated momentum can carry an enterprise forward, for awhile, even if its leaders make poor decisions or loose discipline. Stage 1 [of five stages of decline] kicks in when people become arrogant, regarding success virtually as an entitlement, and they lose sight of the true underlying factors that created success in the first place."

Wow! Do you see the connection between personal and organizational plateauing? I describe arrogance as "trusting in self" with two primary manifestations in plateauing:

1. Self-preservation
2. Self-promotion

Self-preservation tends to be associated with hurt and failure, while self-promotion tends to be associated with ongoing success. Either way, arrogance or "trusting in self" breaks down the faith dynamic so essential in healthy, maturing Christian discipleship and leadership.

Faith Dynamic

Back in the 1980s I was on a church staff that was led by John Wimber, the founder of Vineyard Christian Fellowship. He would occasionally ask us during staff meetings how we spelled faith. His answer was RISK, because he wanted us to understand that faith as a leader involved more that taking care of business. It also involved the dynamics of vision and risk. I agree with this, but have just a little different take on it. I now spell faith TRUST, because I have learned that faith is primarily relational – that taking risks as a leader involves vision that comes from an intimate relationship with God who is able to keep his promises, his way!

Let me explain. Faith (*pistis*) according to Vine (*Vine's Complete Expository* Dictionary, p. 222) means:

> "'firm persuasion,' a conviction based upon hearing (akin to peitho, 'to persuade'), is used in the NT always of 'faith in God or Christ, or things spiritual.' The word is used of (a) **trust**... (b) trust-worthiness... (c) the contents of belief... (d) assurance... (e) a pledge of fidelity... **The main element of 'faith' is its relationship to the invisible God...**"(bold added for emphasis)

According to the author of Hebrews, "faith is being sure of what we hope for and certain of what we do not see" (Hebrews 11: 1, NIV). We also know that "without faith it is impossible to please God..." (Hebrews 11: 6a, NIV). Abraham is used in Hebrews 11 as one of the primary examples of faith and faithfulness in the Old Testament. In a parallel passage in Romans we are given an inside view of Abraham's faith:

> "Against all hope [he was old and his wife was barren]... he did not waver through unbelief regarding the promise of God [for a son], but was strengthened in his faith and gave glory to God, being **fully persuaded that God had power to do what he promised.**" Romans 3: 18-21, NIV (**bold** added for emphasis)

Let me show you how this works in the following diagram that I call the "faith/vision cycle."

We start with revelation (Bible insights and/or hearing the voice of God) and begin to step out in faith (obedience). Done deal, right? No, it does not seem to work that way. I have learned that with faith (obedience) will come resistance. Personally, resistance may come from our flesh, the world, or the enemy. As a leader, resistance may come from these as well as from the people you are leading. Either way, in all likelihood, you will experience resistance as you progress in faith.

Diagram 2: Faith/Vision Cycle

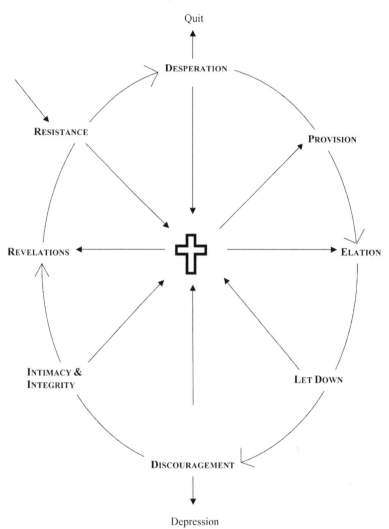

If we continue in faith (obedience), eventually we will see God's provision. Often times, God's provision comes when we are at the end of our own confidence, resources, or abilities. This is because God wants us to learn to live and lead by faith. He wants us to learn how to experience what I call "supernatural natural living". Remember Paul's words about weakness and strength (II Corinthians 12: 10)?

Notice on the diagram that there are two primary points at which we tend to be most vulnerable to giving up or giving in: desperation and discouragement. Desperation can lead to self-doubt that can lead to quitting – "it is just too hard." We do not have the resources to keep going, so we quit. It is at this point where our paradigm is challenged and we can learn how to rely on God's faithfulness to provide!

The second point of vulnerability occurs after we have experienced God's faithful provision. We are initially energized (elated) by seeing God come through. We were hot wired by God for this kind of faith and it is awesome. "Yes! Praise God, I was made for this!!!!" But we, in our humanity, cannot stay here for very long. There will eventually be a let down and we can become vulnerable to discouragement (see the story of Elijah in I Kings 19 for an example of this). Discouragement can lead to self-pity that can lead to full on depression if we are not careful.

In both cases, the primary issue for us to learn to deal with is the weakness of our humanity (self or flesh) and we need to learn how to rely upon God for intimacy and integrity that can lead to further or future revelation and the cycle starts all over again. That is why Paul talks about faith leading to faith (Romans 1: 17). Today's faithfulness is prerequisite for tomorrow's challenges! Faith (trust) is dynamic and leads to personal transformation and a deeper understanding of who God is and how he works.

Checking Our Foundations For "Trust Cracks"

All of us are prone to deny, rationalize, project, and settle for formula instead of learning how to live from faith to faith (Romans 1: 17).

These defense mechanisms are subtle and often times acceptable in our culture, even in the Christian sub-culture.

Over time this defensive posture will betray the reality that we are living and leading in our own strength rather than submitting to God in faith. By default, our defense mechanisms betray the fact that we are trusting in ourselves rather than God. If we do not break this pattern, we will eventually find ourselves stuck in our circumstances and the subtle, but devastating consequences of plateauing will begin to define our lives and leadership and our impact in the organizations that we are apart of.

Trust cracks feed the pattern of self-preservation and self-promotion that is at the core of plateauing. Let's take a closer look at what I mean by trust cracks.

Sources ("Trust Cracks") of Plateauing

Again, the Bible gives us insight and wisdom concerning the "trust crack" that can develop in our spiritual formation foundation that can lead to plateauing. James describes two type of wisdom: heavenly and earthly wisdom. Let's take a closer look at what James has to say about these two types of wisdom. He wrote:

> "Who is wise and understanding among you? Let him show it by his good life, by deeds done in the humility that comes from wisdom. But if you harbor bitter envy and selfish ambition in your hearts, do not boast about it or deny the truth. Such 'wisdom' does not come down from heaven but is earthly, unspiritual, of the devil." (James 3: 13-15, NIV)

So, there are two types of wisdom that have different sources, and eventually, different outcomes. Let's look at the source and outcomes of these.

1. *Heavenly Wisdom's source is God's truth* (verse 14) and its outcomes are (verses 17-18):

* Pure
* Peace-loving
* Considerate
* Submissive
* Full of mercy
* Good fruit
* Impartial
* Sincere

2. *Earthly Wisdom's source is the devil* (verse 15) and its outcomes are (verses 14-16):

* Bitter envy
* Selfish ambition
* Boastful
* Unspiritual
* Disorder
* Evil practice

This is quite a contrast. It may take a long time for the differences in these two types of wisdom to manifest, but eventually they will (see Galatians 6: 7-8). Over the years, I have learned from my own experience and that of others that there are major trust cracks that we need to be aware of and counteract by God's grace if we are to avoid plateauing and manifest the heavenly wisdom that James talked about. These include:

* **Failure** – Everyone experiences failure from time to time, but repeated failure, humiliating failure, or the hurts associated with failure can build up and caused doubts, diminished self-confidence, and ultimately a lack of trust in God. It is easy for most of us to focus on the negative feelings,

perceptions, and consequences associated with failure. We feel like we did something wrong, or are inadequate in some way, or have let others down. All of this can be a pretty heavy load to bear. But there is more to failure than this for those who have faith. John Maxwell calls it "failing forward." I like this concept because it reminds us that God can do something in and through us regardless of our weakness, inadequacies, or even laziness. We can learn from our mistakes and grow in grace and effectiveness.

* **Rejection** - This can be a real time bomb for leaders because it attacks the very core of who we are. Most of us struggle with some sort of insecurity. We have a vague sense that we are worthless (or at least not as valuable in God's eyes as other more talented or successful leaders). This may manifest itself in lack of initiative or trying too hard which can put other people off. We get rejected, which reinforces our poor self-concept, and we can begin to live with the expectation that sooner or later we will be rejected again because of our deficiencies as a person. This is more than a performance issue – it relates to our sense of value. Again, God's intention is to value us through his love and grace so that we can experience his love and love others. This is difficult for many of us to experience because we have been rejected by significant others, especially if they are Christians. How can we trust God if we cannot trust his people? Fortunately, God is not like some of his people. He loves us no matter what and there is self-worth and fulfillment in living in his acceptance!

* **Deep Processing** - J. Robert Clinton, in his *Clinton's Biblical Leadership Commentary*, defines deep processing as "process items which intensively work on deepening the maturity of a leader" (p. 684). Process items involve life circumstances and relationships that result in character development, skill

development, and expanded potential. They are providential in nature, designed by God to help develop a leader's capacity.

Deep processing is a special category of Clinton's list of process items, but they may overlap with other process items in the complexities of life and leadership experiences and relationships. For our purposes here, I have adapted Clinton's findings and come up with the following list of deep processing items:

* Life transitions
* Life and leadership crises
* Life and leadership conflict
* Leadership backlash
* Isolation
* Spiritual warfare
* Brokenness

These deep processing items and the benefits of deep processing will be described in the next chapter (Chapter 6: Deep Processing).

* Success – Too much success and premature promotion can be deadly for faith. We can begin to take ourselves more seriously than we should and gradually think that we have it all figured out or are somehow critical to God's purposes. This is dangerous ground to be on! Sooner or later, our foundation will be exposed. If we have built success on formula or the force of our personality and gifts, we will be exposed for our shallowness and lack of mature substance. Learning how to be faithful in difficult times (deep processing) can be good for us and save us from the frustration and failure of self-promotion.

* Security Issues - Living by sight, rather than by faith, can lead to materialism – a dependence on position, power, popularity, or possessions for a sense of well-being. If our security is not based in our relationship with God we will tend to play it safe or act in our own interests. Over time, we can find ourselves buying into and maintaining a status quo that is compromised at best and spiritually deadly at the worst. It is good to have to trust God for provision, productivity, and his promises. As we do, we grow in our trust and confidence that he is able to keep his promises!

For more information about plateauing and deep processing see the Resouce section in the back of this book. Plateauing is covered more thoroughly in our book *Living and Leading Well* and deep processing is covered in detail in Paul's workbook *Deep Processing: Maturing Through Really Hard Times*.

Gideon: Failure to Move from Fleece to Faith

Text: "Gideon made the gold into an ephod, which he placed in Ophrah, his town. All Israel prostituted themselves by worshipping it there, and it became a snare to Gideon and his family." (Judges 8: 27)

Context: Gideon became a Judge in Israel after seven years of oppression at the hands of the Midianites (Judges 6: 1-6) because Israel "cried to the Lord because of Midian" (6:7). He defeated the Midianites and there was peace in Israel for forty years (8: 28). After he died, the Israelites quickly returned to Baal worship (8: 33).

Overview of Gideon's life and leadership:

* Gideon ("feller, hewer, smiter") was the least in the weakest clan of the tribe of Manasseh (Judges 6: 15)

Starting Well

* He was visited by an angel while threshing wheat in a winepress to keep it from the Midianites (6: 11)
* The angel called Gideon a "mighty warrior" because God was with him (6: 12)
* The Lord commissioned Gideon to: "save Israel out of Midian's hand" (6: 14)
* Gideon asked for a sign (6: 17) and God miraculously provided fire as confirmation (6: 21)
* Gideon built an alter, cut down an Asherah pole for fire wood, and sacrificed a bull (6: 25-27)
* The men of Gideon's town confronted him about this, but his father defended him (6: 28-32)
* While the Midianites, Amalekites, and others joined together to attack Israel (6: 33), the Spirit of the Lord came upon Gideon and he called the Israelites together to defend themselves (6: 34-35)
* While waiting for them to arrive, Gideon asked God for a "fleece" twice as confirmation that God was with him (6: 36-4)
* The Lord had Gideon reduce the size of his army until there were only 300 left (7: 6-7) and armed them with torches, jars, and trumpets (7: 16)
* The Lord woke Gideon up one night and had him go down to the edge of the Midianite camp where he overheard a man telling another about a dream that Gideon would defeat them (7: 13-14)
* Gideon and his 300 men defeated the Midianites (7: 21-8: 21)
* The Israelites asked Gideon to rule them (8: 22) but he refused (8: 23)
* Instead, Gideon asked for gold earrings from the plunder (8: 24)
* They gave Gideon over seventeen hundred shekels (8: 26) of jewelry from which he made a gold Ephod (8: 27) that the Israelites worshipped (8: 27)

* The Ephod became as snare for Gideon and his family (8: 27)
* After Gideon died, the Israelites quickly returned to Baal worship (8: 33) and did not show kindness to Gideon's family (8: 35)

Lessons from the life of Gideon:

1. Gideon viewed himself as insignificant, but was open to God's purpose as a deliverer.

2. Gideon had immature faith and needed a lot of confirmation (sign, two fleeces, and a dream) to obey God.

3. Ultimately, Gideon obeyed God and saw a great victory over the Midianites.

4. Gideon probably showed false humility by refusing the offer to rule Israel, but asking instead for gold. Gold was a source of wealth and power.

5. Gideon's insecurity probably caused him to build the Ephod (symbol of God's anointing) that the Israelites worshipped.

6. Gideon never moved from the fleece (immature faith) to faith (mature trust) in God's ongoing provision.

7. After his death the Israelites returned to idolatry and mistreated his family. He did not leave a lasting legacy.

Now that we have a basic understanding of plateauing, let's take a look at boundaries and their importance for finishing well and establishing a lasting legacy.

Boundaries

In the Introduction to this book, I gave you a basic overview of leadership emergence theory (LET) and the six stages that leaders must pass through successfully if they want to finish well. In this section, we will take a look at the three primary life and leadership boundaries that leaders must navigate as they move towards convergence and finishing well using Terry Walling's reframing of J. Robert Clinton's boundary concept (using the word transition instead of boundaries).

Terry Walling, *Stuck: Navigating the Transitions of Life and Leadership*, has identified three major life and leadership transitions (boundaries) and four stages through each transition (from his study of Clinton's leadership emergence theory). These three transitions (p. XII) are:

1. **Awakening** transition (usually occurring in the 20-30s age range)

2. **Deciding** transition (usually occurring in the 45+ age range)

3. **Finishing** transition (usually occurring in late 50s or early 60s age range)

Each of these transitions (boundaries) is characterized by "a prolonged period of restlessness, self-doubt, lack of motivation, job stagnation, diminished confidence, lack of direction, distance from God, isolation, relational conflict and tension, lack of effectiveness, and struggle to stay focused and motivated" (p. 8). Let's take a closer look at the primary purposes for each of these transitions:

Awakening transition - The primary purposes that God initiates during this transition (which generally takes place during the inner-life growth stage) include (adapted from Walling, p. 65-66):

- The surfacing of past issues that need forgiveness and healing

- The surfacing of passion and potential for leadership and ministry

- The establishing of commitment and an initial understanding of life purposes

- The shaping of character (being) and influence (spiritual authority)

- The establishing of healthy accountability relationships

- The launching of a lifelong journey to experience all God has in store

Deciding transition - The primary purposes that God initiates during this transition (which generally takes place during the ministry/leadership stage) include (adapted from Walling, p. 77-78):

- The further surfacing of past issues that need forgiveness and healing

- The discovery of uniqueness and life message

- The identification of core values

- The further clarification of calling

- The identification of unique leadership methodology based on gift mix and purpose

- The initial insights necessary for living intentionally (focused living)

Finishing transition - The primary purposes that God initiates during this transition (which generally takes place during the life maturing and convergence stages) include (adapted from Walling, p. 87):

- The further surfacing of past issues that need forgiveness and healing

- The clarification of unique calling and commitment to its fulfillment

- The discovery of humility and brokenness as a primary influence base for life transformation

- The commitment to intentionality for focused living

- The discover and determination to fulfill unique ultimate contributions and lasting legacy

- The empowering of others (especially younger emerging leaders) through spiritual authority

During these transitions, we have an invitation to go deeper in our relationship with God that will result in us being better prepared for future challenges and opportunities. Walling describes four stages that we must work through in order to gain the maximum benefit from these major life and leadership transitions:

1. Entry
2. Evaluation
3. Alignment
4. Direction

Entry stage - This stage can take us by surprise. Sometimes it comes gradually and at other times it may come suddenly. Either way, we find ourselves in a situation where what worked yesterday does not seem to work today. What we enjoyed yesterday is not as fulfilling today. How we viewed ourselves yesterday is not how we see ourselves today. Something has changed and there is no going back (even though we may want to and try to).

Evaluation stage - Entry is disorienting, but it can lead to a time of soul searching and an honesty that opens us up for deeper evaluation of our life and leadership. If we can take our disorientation to God, sooner or later, he will begin to reveal to us new insights about ourselves that can lead to greater freedom, clarity, focus, and intentionality (Walling, p. XV). The critical issue here is submitting to God rather than trying to get out of the transition.

As leaders, we are problem solvers. We make things happen. We have a tendency to try and get out of these times of transition through our own devises, but we need to be careful here. By making something happen we may miss God's greater purposes. We need discernment here. Wise counsel, a mini-retreat, or a time of fasting and prayer might be in order to better discern if God is initiating a major life or leadership transition (or something else is going on). We do not want to miss out on what God can do in these times of major transitions by trying to take a short cut!

Alignment stage - This stage occurs when we have heard from God about his purpose(s) in this life or leadership transition and we are willing to submit to him. This may involve dealing with deep-seated issues in our lives or a major transition in role or location. Usually, there is a process of dying to our selfishness that takes place as we align ourselves with God's purpose(s).

Evaluation and alignment may loop back and forth several times over a prolonged period of time, especially if we are resistant to God's dealing with us. Usually, you will experience several cycles of evaluation and alignment during major transitions. The shortest, least painful way to move through major transitions is to open your heart to God and cooperate with him in doing his deeper work of transformation.

Direction stage - Out of alignment we can gain a greater, clearer sense of direction. We may have to wait on God longer than we are comfortable with, but the wait will be worth it. God will open up new opportunities and fulfill his promises in ways that give him glory and increase our faith and effectiveness as a person and leader.

Thomas – Boundaries and Doubting

Text – "Unless I see the nail marks in his hands and put my finger where the nails were, and put my hand into his side, I will not believe it." John 20: 25, NIV

Context: Thomas ("twin") was one of the Twelve called to be with Jesus (Matthew 10: 3, Mark 3: 18, Luke 6: 15). He is not mentioned by name in the Synoptic gospels after being listed as one of the Twelve. He is mentioned by name in the Gospel of John (seven times) and Acts (once).

Overview of Thomas' Life and Ministry:

* He was involved in Jesus' Mentoring>Empowering>Multiplication (M>E>M) strategic training of the Twelve (for more information about this see Chapter 11: Passing the Baton)
* Thomas was involved in the discussion about Lazarus' death – John 11: 16
* He was involved in a discussion about Jesus' imminent crucifixion – John 14: 5
* He abandoned Jesus during his arrest and trial – Matthew 26: 31
* Thomas witnessed the events of the crucifixion – John 19
* He was absent when Jesus appeared to his disciples after his resurrection – John 20: 19, 24
* Thomas does not believe the other disciple's report that they had seen Jesus – John 20: 24

* A week later, Jesus appears to the disciples again. This time Thomas is with them. Jesus confronts Thomas and has him put his finger in the nail hole and his hand in his side – John 20: 26-27
* Jesus also exhorts Thomas to stop doubting and believe and he responds, "My Lord and my God!" – John 20: 27-28
* Thomas went fishing with Peter and other disciples and witnessed a miraculous catch and the restoration of Peter – John 21
* He was in the upper room with the 120 believers to pray and wait for the promised coming of the Holy Spirit – Acts 1: 8, 12-15

<u>Lessons from Thomas:</u>

1. You can be in, but not all the way in. Thomas was committed enough to follow Jesus, but struggled along the way with doubts and insecurities.

2. There is legitimate doubt and faith killing doubt. It is O.K. to doubt, question, and struggle as long as you can trust in the integrity of God as loving, sovereign, and able to keep his promises.

3. Doubts, even faith killing doubts, do not have to be the end of the story. We can wrestle through our doubts and come back to faith in God. In the case of faith killing doubt we will need to confess this as sin and repent by exercising trusting faith in God.

4. Doubt can lead to a greater depth of understanding and relationship with God.

For more information about doubting, see Appendix C: Doubting and Wisdom (from the Book of Job).

Evaluation and Application Questions

1. What is the definition of plateauing? Boundaries? Why is establishing, maintaining, and enlarging our foundation of faith (TRUST) important for navigating the challenges of mid-life if we want to finish well? How would you rate your faithfulness? What areas do you need to improve and how are you going to go about it?

2. What did you learn about plateauing? Boundaries? What did you learn about faith dynamics? What insights have you gained that will help you remain faithful in your personal life and organizational leadership?

3. What trust cracks did you discover in your foundation? If you have any, how are you going to repair them?

4. How are you doing in navigating your personal boundaries? What are the specific area(s) that you are vulnerable? How are you going to strengthen these areas and guard yourself from becoming more vulnerable?

5. What did you learn from studying the life of Gideon? Thomas? What lessons do you need to apply to your own life and how do you plan to do so?

Chapter 6

Deep Processing

James reminded Christians who were being persecuted for their faith to:

> "Consider it pure joy, my brothers [and sisters], whenever you face trials of many kinds, because you know that the testing of your faith develops perseverance. Perseverance must finish its work so that you may be mature and complete, not lacking anything." James 1: 2-4, NIV

As leaders, we are already aware that we have had, are currently, or will face a variety of life situations that fall into James' concept of "trials of many kinds." What we need to be reminded of is that these trials have a purpose and can produce maturity in our lives and leadership.

Notice that James says that we can have joy in the midst of our trials, because we know that God has a purpose in them. Joy (*chara*) is the filling and overflow of the "fruit" of the Holy Spirit (Galatians 5: 22) in our lives and leadership. This joy has the following qualities:

1. It is relational, not primarily circumstantial.
2. It is volitional, not primarily emotional.
3. It is enduring, not temporary.

We can experience the fruit of the spirit in the midst of our many and various trials, because God is with us (Matthew 28: 20), Jesus modeled it (Hebrews 12: 2), and good things can result from them. James went on in this passage to describe the results of persevering through trials by stating, "that we may be mature and complete, not lacking anything" (James 1: 4, NIV). The promise is that the outcome of trials can be maturity. But, how does this happen?

James used an interesting metaphor to describe the process: "the testing of [our] faith." Testing (*dokimazo*) refers to the process of refining precious metals. A crucible was used to hold raw materials as they were exposed to heat. The raw materials would melt and the impurities would separate to the surface. The impurities would be removed and the process repeated until the precious metals were purified. I have been told that the metal was declared as sterling when the craftsman could see his face reflected in the surface of the molten metal.

What a powerful picture of a leader's relationship with Christ! As we endure life's many and various trials, God is producing Christ-likeness in us so that when we are under pressure we will reflect him in how we navigate our challenging circumstances. The fruit of the spirit will manifest itself in and through us as we mature in the midst of the hardships of life.

The purpose of trials is to help us become more mature by putting us in pressure situations that reveal the impurities of our heart so that we can be transformed by submitting to God in his removal of them. This is why James could say, "Consider it pure joy brother {sisters}, whenever you face trials of many kinds..." (James 1: 2, NIV).

Transformation

The goal of this process is transformation – Christ-likeness. God wants to change us from the inside out. He wants to transform us! Let's take a closer look at how transformation generally takes place by describing the transformational learning cycle:

Diagram 3: Transformational Learning Cycle

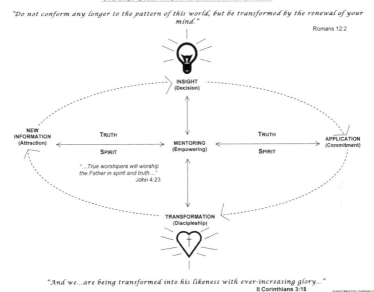

Starting Well

Have you ever wondered why so few people experience long-term change (transformation) through programs, classroom teaching, or even great sermons? People may have momentary insights or even emotional responses, but a few months later they may be right back where they were or even in a worse condition. What is going on with this?

Let me make a distinction here between learning and transformation. Learning is critical to behavior change, but is not the same thing. The Bible makes the distinction between knowledge - knowing truth; wisdom - knowing how to apply truth; and transformation - living in the truth. Learning involves the first two concepts, while transformational learning involves all three.

Note here that the roles of the truth and the spirit are critical in true transformation. Some can change through their own self-will (that can lead to pride and legalism) while others become discouraged by their inability to change (which can lead to condemnation). What we need are the resources necessary for gracious transformation that keep us from either extreme. The Bible promises us freedom and abundance (John 8: 32 and John 10: 10). A good example of this is the fruit of the spirit described in Galatians 5: 22-23. This fruit includes:

- Love

- Joy

- Peace

- Patience

- Kindness

- Goodness

- Faithfulness

- Gentleness

- Self-control

This is what God promises and what many of us want. How, then, do we get this kind of fruit? It comes as a result of transformation. Diagram 3 describes a cycle that starts with new information ("attraction") that can lead to insight. Insight is a new way of looking at ourselves, our situation, or how to approach a problem or challenge. The light bulb goes on and we see something in a new way or to a greater degree.

If this insight is convincing enough or we are desperate enough to make a change ("decision"), we attempt to apply this new understanding to our lives, which can lead to behavioral change ("commitment"). But behavior change does not always reflect heart change, which is the core reality of transformation ("discipleship"). Unless our hearts are changed by the work of the word and the spirit, we are not transformed even though we may be making better behavioral choices in our lives.

I have discovered over time that some transformational changes are easier than others. This is where the empowering of healthy mentoring can help. It generally takes us about three to six months to change behavior and establish new habits through consistent application. Let me illustrate this further from a situation that happened to Shadrach, Meshach, and Abednego (Daniel 3) in the Old Testament.

Faithfulness in the Fire

Shadrach, Meshach, and Abednego were part of the exile in Babylon (Daniel 1: 1-2). They were selected, along with Daniel, for training in government service (Daniel 1: 3-7). They joined Daniel in refusing to defile themselves by eating the unclean food that was available to them during their training (Daniel 1: 8). They worked out a compromise with the King's official concerning their diet (Daniel 1: 9) and ultimately excelled in their training and wisdom (Daniel 1: 19-20). After they completed their training at the top of their class, they entered the King's service (Daniel 1: 19).

In Daniel 3, we read that the King had a giant golden image (possibly of himself) set up and required all his subjects to "fall down and worship it" (Daniel 3: 1-5). Failure to do this was punishable by being immediately thrown into a blazing furnace (Daniel 3: 6). Shadrach, Meshach, and Abednego refused to fall down and worship and they were reported to the King (Daniel 3: 12).

This will date me, but I am a fan of Keith Green. One of his albums was titled "No Compromise" and the cover depicted Shadrach, Meshach, and Abednego standing in the midst of the crowd who had fallen down to worship the image and Royal Guards on horses pointing them out! I have never forgotten that picture of the bravery and faithfulness of these three young men who served God faithfully in the midst of a pagan culture!

But they had to face the fire! God did not intervene at this point. The crowd was not moved by their bravery, the guards did not overlook their act of bravery; the King was not struck with insanity (yet, anyway). No, Shadrach, Meshach, and Abednego had to face the King – and he was not very happy (Daniel 3: 19). In fact, he was so angry with them and their refusal to bow down to him in private (Daniel 3: 15-18) that he ordered the furnace heated seven times hotter than usual (Daniel 3: 19).

Well, you know the rest of the story - Shadrach, Meshach, and Abednego were thrown into the fire, but they were not consumed (Daniel 3: 22-25). In fact, they were seen walking around in the fire with a fourth person who "looks like the son of the gods" (Daniel 3: 25, NIV). Not only this, they were not harmed, singed, scorched, or even have the sent of smoke on them (Daniel 3: 27).

When the King commanded them to come out of the furnace, there was only one change. They had gone in bound and they came out unbound (Daniel 3: 20 and 24-25). What a picture of faithfulness in the fire! We start bound in some way or another and end up free! Not only this, but God was honored (Daniel 3: 28-29) and they got a promotion (Daniel 3: 30). This Old Testament story is an illustration of what James says about trials!

A closer look at this story reveals a progression of faithfulness in the fire leading to what James calls maturity. Let's take a look at this progression:

1. Faithfulness leads to difficulties (Daniel 3: 12).
2. Further faithfulness leads to even greater difficulties (Daniel 3: 15-20).
3. Faithfulness leads to the furnace (Daniel 3: 22-23).
4. Faithfulness leads to intimate fellowship with God (Daniel 3: 24-25).
5. Faithfulness leads to transformation (Daniel 3: 25).
6. Faithfulness leads to supernatural deliverance (Daniel 3: 26-27).
7. Faithfulness leads to glorifying God (Daniel 3: 28-29).
8. Faithfulness leads to greater opportunities for influence (Daniel 3: 30).

Now that we have taken a look at how God refines us through trials, lets look at a specific type of trials called deep processing. For these deeper or more complex issues, the process of maturation and transformation may take longer and be extremely painful.

For these types of issues, we often need a support system to help us break through to transformation. A trusted spiritual mentor can provide support, understanding, encouragement, accountability, prayer, and other resources that can help us keep from giving in or giving up when we fail or life circumstances wear us down. The bottom line is: we need one another!

Deep Processing

J. Robert Clinton, in his *Clinton's Biblical Leadership Commentary*, defines deep processing as "process items that intensively work on deepening the maturity of a leader" (p. 684). Process items involve life circumstances and relationships that result in character development, skill development, or expanded potential. They are providential in nature, designed by God to help develop a leader's capacity.

Clinton has identified over 50 process items in his study of leaders in the Bible. Deep processing involves several of these. For our purposes here, I will briefly describe the following deep processing items that are especially important as me mature and transition into the end game:

- Conflict

- Ministry Conflict

- Crisis

- Life Crisis

- Leadership Backlash

- Isolation

- Brokenness

I add to this list brokenness, although this dynamic is probably integrated into the reality of all deep processing. Before we take a look at brokenness in some detail, let's briefly define and describe the other deep process items. The following definitions are taken from the Glossary in Clinton's *The Making of a Leader*:

1. Conflict – "Instances in a leader's life in which God uses conflict, whether personal or ministry related, to develop the leader in dependence upon God, faith, and insights relating to personal life and ministry" (p. 237).
Example: Joseph (Genesis 37-50)

2. Ministry Conflict – "A process item referring to those instances in ministry in which a leader learns either positive or negative lessons about the nature of conflict, possible ways to resolve conflict, possible ways to avoid conflict, ways to creatively use conflict, and how to see conflict in terms of God's processing of the leader's inner life" (p. 249).
Example: Paul and Barnabas (Acts 15)

3. Crisis – "Process items that refer to special intense situations in life, which are used by God to test and teach dependence on Him" (p. 238).
Example: Daniel (Daniel 6)

4. Life Crisis – "A specialized form of a Crisis process item, referring to a time of crisis characterized by intense pressure in which the meaning and purpose of life are searched out, and the leader has experienced God in a new way as the Source of life, the Sustainer of life, and the Focus of life" (p. 246).
Example: Paul (Acts 9)

5. Leadership Backlash – "A process item describing the condition when followers react against a course of action taken by a leader; usually due to unforeseen complications arising after the followers have previously approved of the action" (p. 245).
Example: Moses (Exodus 14)

6. Isolation – "A maturity factor item in which a leader is separated from normal ministry, while in the natural context in which the ministry has been occurring, usually for an extended time, and thus experiences God in a new and deeper way" (p. 244-245).
Example: Elijah (I Kings 19)

7. **Brokenness** – A process by which God brings us to the end of our self in order for us to learn to live and lead under the control of his spirit. There may be several breakings before brokenness is accomplished. The primary fruit of brokenness is love (I Timothy 1: 5) that is manifest in humility (I Peter 5: 6).
Example: Job (Job 1-42)

Brokenness is a deep processing item and a favorable result of enduring deep processing. Because it is so important for convergence and afterglow, let's take a closer look at a Biblical character that probably best models this type of deep processing.

Job: Brokenness and Blessing

The key to our understanding of brokenness in the life and leadership of Job are found in the following two passages:

- "My spirit is broken..." (Job 17: 1, NIV)

- The Lord blessed the later part of Job's life more than the first..." (Job 42: 12, NIV)

These two passages provide a context for the deep processing that Job experienced and gives us hope that extreme suffering can be purposeful and productive in us and in other's lives. Let's take a closer look at brokenness and blessing in the life of Job.

Job means "object of enmity" and he was "blameless and upright; he feared God and shunned evil" (Job 1: 1). He was "the greatest man among all the people of the East" (Job 1: 3) and he was caring and concerned about his children (1: 4-5).

Suddenly, all of this was put to a test. In one of the few glimpses into the heavenly realm in the Bible, we see an exchange between

Deep Processing

God and Satan (Job 1: 6-12) in which God allowed Satan to bring great suffering upon Job in the form of two tests:

1. The loss of his possessions and children (Job 1: 6-19)
2. The loss of his health and support of his wife (Job 2: 1-9)

In all this, Job did not "sin by charging God with wrongdoing" (Job 1: 22) or "sin in what he said" (Job 2: 10). Not only did he suffer through these circumstances, but he also had to endure the added burden of the counsel and accusations of his friends (Job 3-37):

* Eliphaz (4-5, 15, 22) – if you sin, you suffer/only the wicked suffer
* Bildad (8, 18, 25) – you must be sinning/the wicked always suffer
* Zophar (11, 20) – you are sinning/the wicked are short lived

During this time, Job claimed his integrity throughout his sufferings (Job 2: 3, 9; 27: 5; 31: 6) while complaining that:

* God has failed to hear him (Job 13: 3, 24; 19: 7; 23: 3-5; 30: 20)
* God is punishing him (Job 6: 4; 7: 20; 9: 17)
* God has allowed the wicked to prosper (Job 21: 7)

Fortunately, one of Job's friends listened to his complaints and defense, probably showing him the love that he needed:

* Elihu (32-37) – God purifies and teaches/humble yourself and submit to God

Finally, God spoke and Job answered (Job 38-41). God does not answer Job's questions or address his complaints directly. He showed Job his majesty, which silenced him and allowed him to gain new perspective on who God really was and how he functions. This led Job to humble himself and repent (Job 42: 1-6). Job then offered sacrifices and prayed for his friends (Job 42: 7-10) and then came blessing! God blessed Job with "twice as much as he had before" (Job 42: 10) and a long, fulfilling life (Job 42: 16-17).

What can we learn from the story of Job? Plenty! J. Robert Clinton, in *Clinton's Biblical Leadership Commentary*, has identified a process of brokenness that I have adapted from my own study of Job. The process of brokenness in Job goes something like this:

1. Self pity – "Why me?" (Job 3)
2. Sensitivity to the opinions of others – "You have sinned! Admit it. (Job 4: 1; 5: 17)
3. Personal evaluation – "What have I done to deserve this?"
   a. Personal sin
   b. Paradigm challenge
4. Sense of brokenness – despair, discouragement, depression (Job 6: 12-14)
5. Honest complaining/questioning of God – "Why is this happening?" "This is not fair/right?" "What is your purpose in this?" (Job 7: 11)
6. Loss of felt presence of God - "Who/Where are you?" (Job 13: 21; 23: 3)
7. Broken spirit – end of self resources (Job 17: 1; also see Psalms 34:18)
8. Humility and submission – trust regardless of circumstances (Job 42: 2)
9. Repentance and compassion – turning away from self and toward God and others (Job 42: 6-9)

10. Restoration and double blessing – prosperity and blessing (Job 42: 10-17)

If there is blessing in brokenness, why do so few of us submit to the process? I have discovered two primary barriers to brokenness in my study of Job. They are:

1. Bitterness – "curse God…" (2: 9)
2. Self pity – "… and die." (2: 9)

These two barriers seem to separate those of us who are transformed through brokenness and those who get lost in their pain and confusion. God never seems to give Job an explanation for what he went through. There does not seem to be any sense of fairness in Job's experience. In fact, Job's suffering seem unfair and even brutal. How can a loving God allow such suffering? I do not know, but I have learned through my own experiences with brokenness that God is loving (Romans 8: 35-39), merciful (in a severe way), sovereign, and able to do "immeasurable more than all we can ask or imagine, according to his power that is at work within us…" (Ephesians 3: 20, NIV).

The bottom line here is: Can we really trust God to do good in spite of our pain and confusion? Faith in these times is spelled TRUST! He is trustworthy (or we are in big trouble)! Bruce Wilkinson, in *A Life God Rewards*, reminds us of some of the blessings of brokenness. He lists several:

1. Brokenness humbles us (Job 22: 29)
2. Brokenness tests us (Job 2: 3)
3. Brokenness rearranges our priorities (Job 42: 5-6)
4. Brokenness disciplines us (Job 5: 17)
5. Brokenness prepares us for future blessings (Job 42: 10)

What can we learn from the life of Job? J. Robert Clinton, in *Clinton's Biblical Leadership Commentary*, has identified the following helpful lessons:

1. Defend God at all costs – He can be trusted even when we do not understand (Job 42: 2).

2. Spiritual warfare is part of faithfulness in leadership (Job 1-2).

3. Be open to paradigm shifts and recognize that a major cause is experiential conflict (Job 42: 5).

4. Brokenness is a major means to developing new paradigms and preparing us for future blessings (Job 17: 1; 42: 10-17).

5. God is with us in and through our times of testing/suffering and will accomplish his purpose(s) (Job 42: 2, 5, 10-17).

This leads us to one of the most important blessings of brokenness - The release of the spirit for much fruit in life and leadership (John 15: 5). The key to much fruit in this passage is abiding through "much pruning."

The Release of the Spirit

Watchman Nee, in *The Breaking of the Outer Man and the Release of the Spirit*, is very helpful for our understanding of brokenness. There is a rich, but under utilized tradition of writings on brokenness. Probably the most well known writing on this subject is *Dark Night of the* Soul by Saint John of the Cross. But I like Nee. I have found his insights easier to understand and apply. I am aware that some of Nee's theology is suspect, but I have read most of his books and a couple of his biographies and come to the conclusion that his teaching on brokenness and the release of the spirit is basically sound and very insightful.

Deep Processing

It is important to understand the context in which Nee lived and ministered in order to properly assess his writings. Angus Kinnear, in his biography of Nee entitled *Against the Tide*, states (p. ix) that:

> "Watchman Nee personally wrote and published only one book [*The Spiritual Man*], but he left an almost complete record of his sermons, lecture, and conference addresses which were published in several magazines he edited."

He also lived and served in some very difficult circumstances involving civil unrest, an invasion and occupation by the Japanese (WW II), and the eventual take over of Mainland China by Mao and his communist party loyalists. Nee eventually spent years in Communist prison where he was unsuccessfully subjected to Maoist "re-education." All this to say, that understanding the context of his life can help us to better gleam the wisdom of his legacy for understanding the potential blessings of brokenness or what he called "the release of the spirit." Let me share several quotes with you and then give a summary of insights that I have gained from Nee's writing on brokenness:

"When we receive a new spirit [at conversion], we receive God's Spirit at the same time. When our human spirit was revived from its deadened state, we received the Holy Spirit at the same time. The Holy Spirit resides in our spirit, but it is difficult to tell which is the Holy Spirit and which is our spirit. There is a distinction between the Holy Spirit and our spirit, but the two are not separate. Hence, the release of the spirit is not merely a release of man's spirit but a release of the Holy Spirit through man's spirit, because the two spirits are one" (p. 18-19).

"When the outer man is broken, the spirit will be open and free to flow to others, and when the spirit is open and free, others can easily touch it" (p. 22).

"Those who are broken by the Lord will find that their outer man no longer influences their inner man. They can take care of outward things with their outer man, while at the same time continue to abide in God and in his presence" (p. 28).

"God does not destroy our outer man. But neither will he allow it to remain intact and unbroken. He wants to pass through our outer man. He wants our spirit to love, think, and make decisions through the outer man. God's work can only be accomplished through a broken outer man" (p. 36).

"This is the Lord's way. He has to break us before he can have an outlet through us" (p. 40).

The release of the spirit leads to functioning out of spiritual authority as our primary power and influence base. This is critical for our effectiveness in convergence and afterglow. Without spiritual authority a leader is limited in both influence and effectiveness.

Spiritual Authority

Clinton, in *The Making of a Leader*, has identified 10 commandments of spiritual authority that he drew from Nee's book, *Spiritual Authority*, which compliments Nee's teaching on brokenness. It is out of brokenness that we experience a release of the spirit resulting in spiritual authority to cooperate with God in his transforming, kingdom expanding work. The following characteristics are adapted from Clinton's list of "Ten Commandments of Spiritual Authority" (p. 102):

1. One who learns spiritual authority as a primary base for leadership recognizes God as the primary source of all life changing authority.

2. Spiritual authority is delegated by God and those who exercise it do so in humility.

3. The leader who exercises spiritual authority is responsible to God for how he uses it.

4. The leader who exercises spiritual authority is also sensitive to its use in others and in real-life situations.

5. Subjection to a leader exercising spiritual authority is ultimately submission to God.

6. Leaders functioning in spiritual authority are not perfect leaders. Refusal to submit to them for personal, style, competency, etc. reasons may actually be rebellion (against God).

7. Leaders who exercise spiritual authority are sensitive to God's authority in others and willing to submit themselves when appropriate.

8. Spiritual authority is never exercised for one's own benefit. It is always exercised for the benefit of others.

9. A leader who exercises spiritual authority does not insist on or manipulate followers to submit. Followers will recognize God's presence and power and willingly submit.

10. God will defend leaders who are consistently functioning out of spiritual authority.

These characteristics of spiritual authority are critical in a leader who experiences convergence in life and leadership and is the basis for passing the baton on to the next generation of leaders.

Application and Discussion Questions:

1. What have you learned about deep processing from reading this chapter?

2. Which of the deep processing process items have you experienced? What did you learn from these experiences?

3. What is your understanding of brokenness? What is your experience with brokenness? What have you learned about it so far?

4. What is your take on Nee's teaching on brokenness and the release of the spirit?

5. Why is spiritual authority important for finishing well in life and leadership? What is your assessment of your influence base as a leader?

Chapter 7

Renewal

The Man in the Front Row

"Young man, slow down. You are talking too fast and I can't write it all down!" I (Richard) will never forget the time I heard those words. I was with my father and we were teaching on leadership development to a group of pastors in Malaysia. We were meeting in a special Christian retreat center built on a mountainside. What made this experience so memorable was not the fact that I was talking too fast. What made it memorable was the old man who was sitting in the front row. He was the one who made the comment. What made it so meaningful to me was the story of his life.

Being a Christian leader in a Muslim nation is not easy. Being an effective Christian leader who planted a large church that spawned a church planting movement was really not easy. Being used by God to catalyze so many incredible impacting ministries was really not easy. Buying land and building a Christian retreat center in a location dedicated to idolatrous worship and recreation was really not easy. But the man sitting in the front row had experienced the powerful presence of God over his lifetime and God enabled him to be the leader who did all those things. This was the man who was asking me to slow down. I slowed down.

Besides slowing down, I did another thing; I resolved in my heart that I would do everything within my power to be just like him when I got to be his age. I resolved to stay humble and most of all, I resolved to stay hungry to learn. This man was such a powerful model of so many things that I wanted in my life. He was a leader who was finishing well and demonstrated a vibrant relationship to God. He was such an encouragement to leaders around him. And he really wanted to keep learning at a time when others might be tempted to lean back and relax. This attitude and these actions are what help leaders in the end game experience the renewal that they need to finish well. A healthy learning posture is what is needed to stay in the game and be renewed with fresh energy and power to keep going God's way in the end game.

What is Renewal for a Leader?

Over the years that we have been studying leaders and the concept of finishing well, we have developed a list of things that enhance our chances of finishing well. One of the things on the list is what we call renewal experiences. We have observed in leaders who have finished well that they had a number of renewal experiences over the course of their life. These experiences are unique to each individual. God uses a wide variety of situations, circumstances, and people to bring renewal to his leaders.

As we analyzed all of the different kinds of experiences, we begin to understand what renewal is all about. My father (J. Robert Clinton, lecture on renewal in the lives of Abraham and Daniel) has developed the following definition of renewal. He describes it like this, "Renewal is an especially meaningful encounter with God in which he communicates with *freshness* various kinds of things needed by a leader such as:

- Insights about himself,

- Affirmation—both personal and ministry,

- Inspiration to continue,

- Breakthrough concepts that inspire one to try them in ministry,

- A sense of his personal presence and/or power,

- An unusual sense of intimacy can be tied to some symbolic thing (like a place, physical object, etc.),

- Perspective on time, now or the future so that one's faith is increased to see God in what is happening and will happen, so as to give the leader another anchor upon which to build a sense of a new start, a beginning again, and a desire to rededicate and continue on in following God. "

I want to take this definition and break it down so that we can capture the essence of what renewal is all about. First of all, it is *an encounter with God*. Renewal happens through encounters with God. The encounter can be direct or indirect. It can come through a wide variety of situations, circumstances, and through a variety of different people. But behind all of these is God. A renewal experience is with God.

Secondly, it is *a special encounter*. The encounter does something to us. Hopefully, we are encountering God on a daily basis, but a renewal experience is something that causes something to happen inside of us. My dad describes this as an experience that provides an anchor in our lives. What he means by this is that the leader walks away from the encounter and identifies or knows that this encounter with God is something that will hold them in place. It will be an anchor in the sense that when the storms of life rage, what God did or communicated to us will be something that we can hold on to and it will be something that will keep us from being blown away.

Thirdly, the result of the encounter with God will lead us to *a sense of beginning, a new starting point, a sense of rededication* in our walk with God. It will provide a sense of freshness in us. It may not be something new to us, but the encounter with God will be fresh. This is why the old man on the front row impressed me. He was hungry for an encounter with God. I do not think that there was anything that I was going to say that was new for him, but he was hungry for an encounter with God. That was what caught my attention.

Fourthly, if you look at all the different kinds of experiences that lead to renewal, you can see that leaders need *a lot of different kinds* of encounters with God along the way. Renewal encounters cannot be limited to one kind of encounter. This means that leaders need to be aware that they will need to stay open to different kinds of situation and people. Many renewal encounters with God will come through something that is a bit out of the ordinary for that leader.

Three Categories of Renewal Encounters

From this definition of renewal in the lives of the leaders in the Bible, we were able to identify three general categories of renewal experiences. There may be other categories, but these are the three that we have identified from our studies so far.

The first category of renewal encounter is called *Need Centered*. Need centered renewal encounters are those encounters that are needed because of what is going on in the life of the leader.

Often, there is some kind of crisis in the leader's life or ministry that creates the need for an encounter with God. The external circumstances create an internal need within the leader to encounter God. The need to experience the reality of God in the situation is what drives this category of renewal encounters. The leader needs to know, feel, understand, or see God in the situation.

In the life of Daniel, we see a number of situations where Daniel was in a crisis. Many of these crises come from circumstances outside of Daniel's control. In these experiences, Daniel needed to encounter God's presence and power. His life was being threatened. These circumstances lead Daniel into encounters with God that brought renewal and encouraged him to maintain his integrity, his commitment to Yahweh, and to have hope for Israel's return to their homeland.

A second category of renewal experience is called *Surprises of God*. In this type of renewal experience, the leader may not be aware of their need for a renewal encounter. God intervenes in the normal daily life situations and brings a renewal experience to the leader. These kinds of experiences of renewal can come through the normal ministry efforts of the leader.

God shows up in a special way, as we are obedient to God in our daily affairs. The result is a big boost in confidence and affirmation in our understanding of God, ministry, and faithfulness. Also, God can show up and interrupt our normal routines that can lead to new perspectives or paradigms. Gideon is an example of this. He was going about his business and surprised when God showed up. Even though Gideon was not looking for God, God was looking for Gideon and wanted to know if he was willing to step up into a greater leadership role in Israel.

A third category of renewal encounters is called *Specially Sought*. In this category, the leader is aware of their need for a touch from God and they seek it. They focus on seeking God and look for his intervention. We know that over the course of a leader's lifetime, they will run into times of dryness, times of ruts and routines, and times of crises and conflict. It is in these times that we know that we need to experience a touch of renewal from God. Leaders often use spiritual disciplines and times of retreat to help them focus on God. The disciplines of abstinence are often used to help focus the leader. Daniel entered into a time of fasting and prayer expecting God to come and reveal himself. Jesus himself often withdrew and isolated himself in order to connect with his Father. These are just a few of numerous examples of how leaders have sought God and experienced renewal through exercising spiritual disciples or times of retreat.

Keys to Experiencing Renewal in the End Game

There are a number of issues that we may face in the end game that influences our experiences of renewal. These issues are common to many of us and we may have to face them one way or another. Every leader lives in a setting of people, circumstances, and situations that are unique to them. But there are issues common to all of us. These include:

1. The Potential Distraction of the "New"

As I get older, I have noticed that Solomon's words have become more and more true. He says in Ecclesiastes 1: 9, "What has been will be again, what has been done will be done again; there is nothing new under the sun." This is especially true when we consider that God is the same yesterday, today, and forever. This dynamic creates one of the challenges we have to overcome in the end game.

To stay fresh and experience renewal, we need to find new ways to learn known things. I think this is one of the keys to making it through the end game. Solomon was right about nothing being "new under the sun." Trying to find the new is not the basis of maintaining a vibrant growing posture towards learning. In our

Western culture we are too enamored with the new, the next trend or fad. This is especially true when it comes to our efforts to grow and develop effectiveness in ministry.

One of the things that can help keep us fresh is seeing how God wants to apply something known to new contexts. There are many things we can learn that have already been done by people who have gone before us. While God is the same and there is nothing new under the sun, the context of ministry and culture is constantly changing. This means that we need fresh ways to communicate and apply what we have learned. This pursuit can aid us in experiencing renewal as we wrestle with how to communicate and minister in new contexts.

In addition to new contexts, we change as we mature and grow older. We learn things along the way. We grapple with issues that force us to go deeper. We face changing ministry experiences that often force us to go deeper. I have had the experience many times of learning more or going deeper.

Base + Advance

My father has developed an approach to learning and developing as a teacher and communicator called "base + advance". He suggests that we force ourselves to grow and learn by not teaching the same things the same ways. If you have been in ministry for a long time, you know that we often teach the same or similar things over and over.

My father was a professor for nearly 30 years. He taught some of his classes more than twenty-five times. What he tried to do was grow, learn and add new things each time he taught. His strategy was to take what he had compiled already, his "base," and "advance" the material by adding new things he was learning (content) or adding new techniques for communicating them. Using an approach like this will greatly enhance our chances of experiencing a touch of renewal as God expands our understanding.

2. Passing On the Baton

In the end game, we are often involved in transferring responsibilities and what we have learned to others. Staying fresh involves learning how to see the ministry context through the eyes of those we are trying to empower. Helping them to grasp the truths, values, and lessons we have learned can help keep us fresh. There can be a tendency to criticize and put down new ministry contexts and new situations and yearn for the "good ole days." This needs to be avoided. This tendency can creep in when the new contexts are changing and are influenced by values and strategies that we cannot comprehend. An important aspect of passing the baton involves explicitly articulating the inner life lessons and values that God has built into us.

The process of articulating these things will give us moments where we can express gratitude and thanks to God for his faithfulness. These moments often serve as opportunities of renewal in our lives. But we do not want to get stuck in the past. What makes this experience even more powerful is trying to articulate what we have learned in the form of values, principles, or lessons for another generation and helping them learn to apply these to other ministry contexts and different cultures. This is where we can experience an energizing touch from God. He has designed us to pass on what we have learned, what we have experienced with God to others. This is part of God's overall redemptive plan. This is especially true when we pass on what we have experienced with God to our families. Paul will talk more about this in Chapter 11: Passing the Baton.

3. Breaking Out of a Rut

Ever get stuck in a rut? The tendency to slow down and allow our spiritual disciplines to erode must be fought off. If we do not fight this off, we can end up in a rut. We can plateau or get stuck in our growth and development. We can get stale unless we make an intentional and deliberate choice to fight off this tendency.

How do we stay motivated in our inner life with God? How do we continue to practice the spiritual disciplines we need in order to fight off this tendency? Many leaders that I know have opened themselves to other spiritual traditions or to new experiences that they find edifying. I have many friends who have turned to historical mentors, leaders from the past to find help. They have turned to spiritual classics (sometimes hundreds of years old) that have helped them break out of ruts they were trapped in. Sometimes old spiritual pathways can provide new and fresh ways of connecting with God. Authors such as Dallas Willard and Richard Foster have helped many leaders to be exposed to sources that have opened up new ways of experiencing God.

Sometimes we will not agree with many of the things that are written or taught by leaders from other traditions, but the experience of working through issues can enhance what we do believe. A key mentor in my life that modeled learning from different sources and different methodologies than the ones they were used to was John Wimber.

Wimber's view was that there is a lot of truth out there that God has revealed. He agreed with the writer of Proverbs (chapter 1), "Wisdom is crying out in the streets." Wimber suggested that what we need to do is learn how to think, reflect, evaluate, and discern truth. Or as he used to say often, "eat the chicken and spit out the bones." His model created in me an attitude that has really helped me to be open to learning from people and experiences that I might have rejected without even checking it out. Because of this, I have experienced a number of powerful renewal experiences along the way.

Inspiration from Four Biblical Leaders

My father introduced me to a leadership exercise that he has picked up along the way. He called it the 'Ultimate Testimony'. We had a little picture of a tombstone. We were asked the question: what would you want people to remember you for? What would you want them to write on your tombstone? Then we had to write what we wanted written on our tombstone. Doing this exercise when I was in my mid 20's made a huge impression on me. I wrote out my ultimate testimony. I have it hanging on the wall in my office. What impressed me the most was what my dad said next about how you reach your goal and live a life that makes this kind of testimony. He said, "Your ultimate testimony is made up of the accumulated average of your daily testimonies." You reach it by living it one day at a time.

In the end game, it is especially important to look at the examples of Biblical leaders who finished well. What can we learn from them? What do we see in their lives that we can apply to our own lives? Let's take a look at four Biblical leaders and see what we can learn from their lives and leadership about finishing well. I will not describe their entire stories, as I want to highlight a few key things that have inspired me concerning finishing well. The issues that I am highlighting are important for us as we make our way through the end game and establish our lasting legacy. They will help us be open to experiencing touches of renewal from God. Just studying their lives and reflecting on their leadership and their personal choices can lead to a touch of renewal.

1. Joshua

Joshua was a special leader in the history of Israel. Probably, no other Biblical leader faced such a unique leadership context. He followed in the footsteps of Moses, arguably the most powerful leader in the history of Israel. But his leadership context was very different from Moses. His task was to lead the people into the Promised Land and conquer it. Then he had to lead the people through dividing and settling the land. He flourished and accomplished the task that was laid out before him.

The following verses are the summary verses about the way Joshua ended his leadership. They reveal what I think are some of the key issues for us. He finished well.

> "But if serving the LORD seems undesirable to you, then choose for yourselves this day whom you will serve, whether the gods your ancestors served beyond the Euphrates, or the gods of the Amorites, in whose land you are living. But as for me and my household, we will serve the LORD." (Joshua 24:15)

> "After these things, Joshua son of Nun, the servant of the LORD, died at the age of a hundred and ten. And they buried him in the land of his inheritance, at Timnath Serah in the hill country of Ephraim, north of Mount Gaash." (Joshua 24: 29-30)

> "Israel served the LORD throughout the lifetime of Joshua and of the elders who outlived him and who had experienced everything the LORD had done for Israel." (Joshua 24: 31)

First of all, Joshua recognized *the importance of personal decisions*. He had seen what happened when Achan made poor decisions and the tragic consequences that effected the whole family. I am sure that this situation was a strong reminder to Joshua of the importance of personal decisions. He also had observed Moses and watched him wrestle with consequences right up until the end. Joshua wanted to finish well and right until the end of his life he wants to be a model of good decision-making for his family and others. His leadership started in his own family. Some of his final words are, "as for me and my family, we will follow the Lord." These words have lived on as one of Joshua's lasting legacies.

Secondly, Joshua recognized *the importance of team building*. He realized that he was not a spiritual leader in the same way that Moses was. He had to build relationships with other spiritual leadership and the priests of Israel and work in cooperation with them. He also recognized that, like Moses, he could not do it all himself. He needed to build a strong leadership team that helped connect him with all the tribal leaders.

The shift from a nomadic lifestyle to settling in cities, towns, and smaller communities was a difficult one. The leadership team that Joshua built was critical to the successful settling of the land. Joshua did this very well and the nation of Israel served the Lord during his lifetime and throughout the lifetimes of the elders that served with Joshua. It is clear that he successfully imparted or embedded the values and lessons that were given to him through Moses to the next generation of leaders.

Thirdly, Joshua understood *the importance of public meetings* and the role they serve in leadership. At the end of his life, he publicly re-affirmed his commitment to serve God and finish well. He had been part of some incredible public meetings and had observed Moses and how Moses used these meetings to build consensus and modeled how to respond to what God was doing. Joshua used this form of meetings with great effect. I think that this kind of public affirmations and re-commitments would help many of us to finish well.

So much of our faith is lived out privately these days and the tendency is to withdraw as we enter the end game. Public events such as conferences, celebrations, and days of remembrance can add a dynamic that I think would be beneficial to many. It brings our level of commitment higher. It gives us a chance to reflect on what has gone on before and a chance to look forward to what is coming. Leaders in the end game are especially poised to be a significant part of this.

These three lessons from Joshua will help us all as we are facing our end game. We all want to finish well. We need to recognize the importance and value of passing on the lessons and values to people around us. We are not on solo journeys. We have to recognize that the personal decisions that we make are important. At the end of our life, we will see that all those daily decisions add up to summarize the overall direction of our life. This is why I think Joshua inspires me so much. He had to live out his leadership first in partnership with Moses and then in Moses' shadow. He lived out his convictions each day at home and in his ministry context. Thank you Joshua for your modeling!

2. Caleb

Caleb inspires me for two reasons. First of all, I am inspired by *his perseverance*. He was a leader who was a part of one of the most crushing disappointments. When the spies came back and persuaded the people to abandon God's plan, Caleb and Joshua were the only ones who put their faith in God. The other ten spies convinced the people to resist God's plan. It resulted in judgment and disaster that lasted 40 years. I can only imagine how difficult this was for Caleb to watch all of his peers die in the desert. How many nights were spent talking about, thinking about and wondering how different things could have been? Talk about dealing with disappointment and frustration.

As difficult as this was, Caleb did not turn from God. He did not get bitter or allow this terrible situation to push him away from God. He did not allow it to lead him into a place of distance and apathy towards God. He stayed focused on staying faithful and he did not allow the 40 years of wandering to turn his heart hard towards God.

I have had to deal with my share of disappointment in ministry. The disappointments that were a result of my decision-making are one kind of disappointment. Those are easier for me to deal with because I can point the finger at myself. I know the way out of that kind of disappointment. The kinds of disappointments that are harder for me to deal with are the ones that result from other people's decisions. They make poor decisions and the ramifications of those decisions create circumstances that affect my ministry context and me. That kind of disappointment is much harder for me. I have to battle the tendency to get jaded, hard hearted, and have to work hard to force myself not to get pessimistic. This is especially difficult when other people's decisions create setbacks and block what I think are God's plans. This has happened on many occasions and I think that it is one of the most difficult aspects of working with people in ministry.

Many times I have wished that I could sit down with Caleb and ask him for some tips, some keys to making it through. His model inspires me that it is possible to make it through. I find myself wondering how the conversations around the campfire with the other leaders and people were. There were probably some world-class complainers and whiners present. How did Caleb deal with all that? How did he protect his own heart? Did he respond with, "I told you so..." or "If only you would have…" Did he consistently point people to God? We do not know, but we do know the end result. Caleb arrived at the edge of the Promised Land surrounded by leaders 40 years younger than him and he was ready. His faith in God was strong and he was ready.

Secondly, *he stayed focused on receiving what God had promised him*. He did not lose his vision, his strength, or his focus. Even in his old age, he stayed focused on the prize, his portion of the Promised Land. This is probably what he is remembered for the most. How many leaders feel the temptation to give up or just give in as they advance in years? How many leaders after facing a crushing setback and disappointment stay focused for four decades? How many of us would do what it took to be ready?

I believe that Caleb' modeling is critical. As leaders, we want to finish in the right place doing the right things. He did not allow anything to distract him. As I get closer to the end game, I want to stay passionate in my pursuit of the things that God has not done yet. I want to continue to pursue God moving forward to be a part of accomplishing the things that I believe God has spoken to me.

One of the things that I do to help myself with this is review on a regular basis what I call my destiny journal. Over the last twenty-five years or so, I have written down in a journal on my computer all of the major experiences where God hinted at or revealed some aspect of his destiny for my life. I believe that God wants us to know what he is doing in our lives and I have been actively pursuing God and asking him to reveal his destiny for me all this time.

The result is that I have about forty major destiny experiences that I have recorded in my journal. On average, I review this journal about every two years. When I was making major decisions in life or ministry, I paid special attention to this journal. Why? I want to see God's destiny for me worked out in my life. I want to make decisions that move me towards accomplishing God's plan for my life.

At this stage of my life as I am moving towards the end game, I can look back over nearly thirty years of ministry and see that much of what God spoke to me about has been or is being accomplished. Many of the things that God revealed about his plan for my life has already happened. But not everything, there is more. God is not finished with me. And the things that God has spoken about or revealed to me are fresh in my mind because I have spent time reviewing my destiny journal in the last year. I want to make decisions that move me towards accomplishing things that I believe God has revealed to me that are not yet accomplished in my life. Caleb's model inspires me to push forward and be ready for God to use me right up until the very end. Thank you Caleb.

3. Daniel

Can you imagine being a part of a situation like Daniel faced in his lifetime? Jerusalem had fallen and he was one of the privileged young men taken from his home, stripped of his status, and forced to go into exile as a slave. Then he faced many life-threatening scenarios during his service to the Babylonian kings. My questions about Daniel are, "How did Daniel stay so passionate and close to God?" "How did he continue to passionately pursue God?" The Bible text does not answer these questions directly, but we know that Daniel was passionate and pursued God throughout his life. Several situations in Daniel's story give us insights into what made him the person he became.

Towards the end of his life, he disciplined himself to pursue God's truth and perspective. He spent time fasting and praying. We know that this was a daily habit and know that there were special times when he sought God in special ways. In addition to this, he had spent time reading and reflecting on the prophecy of Jeremiah. He wanted to know what God was doing and what God's perspective was about what was going on.

Daniel's pursuit of truth and his passion for relationship to God set a high standard for us to emulate. What makes it especially meaningful to me is that Daniel's entire life was lived in the context of having little or no personal control. He lived his whole life in exile as a slave to the Babylonian kings. Sometimes he had incredible prominence and other times he lived in the shadows, seemingly forgotten. Through it all, Daniel stayed focused on building his relationship and his connection to God. His inner life with God was the one thing that he had control over.

Many leaders today do not have a lot of power or control over what happens to them. Circumstances and situations outside of their control set the boundaries for their lives. Financial realities or cultural realities, limited opportunities create boundaries that they cannot break through. Doing leadership within these boundaries is very different than doing ministry in settings where anything is possible and everything can change.

I think Daniel's life powerfully models a kind of spiritual vitality and models how powerful a life lived out for God can be... even in oppressive circumstances. Daniel's influence on followers of God was and still is incredible. His leadership influence is incredible and most of his leadership influence happened after he was dead. His writings... one book... has made an astounding impact. Daniel is one of the greatest Old Testament leaders. Reflecting on Daniel's story and reading what he wrote about himself has inspired me many times.

Daniel's experiences and his character choices under great pressure have made a difference in my life. I deeply desire to be a person of integrity like Daniel. I want to be faithful like Daniel. I want to be a person who disciplines myself to seek the deep and mysterious truths about God and what God is doing in the world. Daniel's story is filled with so many inspirational moments. Spending time in his story has provided countless experiences and encounters with God for me.

4. John

John, the "beloved" was one of the three (along with James and Peter) disciples who Jesus had a special relationship with. His long and faithful life influenced many, but it was not without its challenges. The context of ministry that John faced at the end of his life was one of these challenges. We know from historical records that John had moved from Jerusalem to Ephesus. He had outlived the other apostles and was nearing the end of his life when he was arrested and convicted in the Roman courts.

John was convicted of atheism because he would not bow and worship Caesar as God and Lord. The result was that he was imprisoned on the isle of Patmos off the coast of modern day Turkey. On a clear day, he could see the mainland and his thoughts and prayers were focused on what was happening in the churches that he deeply loved. He had spent his whole life committed to serving Jesus and was a critical leader in building up the church of Jesus Christ.

Now, at the end of his life, imprisoned and separated from the churches he loved, he was hearing reports about what was happening to the churches. The Roman emperor was systematically moving to persecute and destroy the church. But even worse than that, false teachers and prophets had moved into the church and were threatening to destroy it from within. I can only imagine how John was reacting. He had given his whole life to serve Jesus. Was it all for nothing? Was it all going to fall apart?

We know what John did. He cried out to God in prayer. He wanted to know two things: 1. Jesus... where are you? and, 2. What are you doing? Jesus responded one day while John was praying. He showed up, revealed himself, and answered John's questions. He pulled back the curtain and showed John what was really going on. John was given the task of writing down what Jesus revealed to him. Followers of Jesus have benefited from what John wrote down throughout history. The Revelation of Jesus Christ is one of the most dramatic and powerful renewal experiences ever recorded. I can only imagine the effect this experience had on John. What a confirmation of everything that John believed and hoped for in Jesus.

As we enter the end game, we may also face moments where we are under pressure and face severe challenges. We will wonder if everything that we sacrificed and worked for was worth it. We will want to know from God's perspective what he thinks and how he sees it. Until Jesus returns, we know that the enemies of God will be relentless in their attacks. They are committed to destroying and damaging as much as possible of the things of God. They are committed to attacking everything that we have invested our whole lives in.

God, how do you see things? God, how do you evaluate the efforts of my life? God, what is going on? Where are you? What are you doing? These questions will lead us... if we persevere in asking them and if we are patient enough to allow God to answer us in his way and his timing, and if we are open enough and flexible enough to hear God's answers, he will eventually meet us in renewal experiences.

Why? Because these questions will lead us into God's presence. We will encounter him and he will reveal himself. That is one of the things that I take away from John's encounter with Jesus on the isle of Patmos. Jesus revealed himself to John as the kind of person who cares about and wants to respond to these types of questions.

A Few Conclusions

These Biblical examples lead me to a few conclusions. I believe that leaders in this day and age can expect God to do the same things today that he has done for leaders in the Bible. We should expect special moments of intimacy with God. We should expect to receive challenges from God and expect experiences with God where he imparts new vision. We should expect from God experiences of affirmation both for who we are and for the ministry that we are doing. These renewal experiences will not only sustain us and encourage us to keep going, they will make the difference in whether we persevere or not.

I believe that leaders should expectantly look for touches of renewal. We can ask for them. Sometimes God will take the initiative and surprise us. He will lead us into the experiences of renewal that we need. I love it when he does that. What is clear is this: we know that every leader will need to have these experiences of renewal from time to time. In the cases of leaders that we have studied, we have observed that they experienced a major touch of renewal at least four or five times. We need them to stay on track and to stay passionate in our pursuit of God.

There are special times in life during our development as leaders where we need these experiences. Times of transition are one of those times. Frequently during these critical periods it is easy to let our spiritual disciplines slack. There can be a tendency to plateau and rely on one's past experience and skills. There can be a sense of confusion concerning our achievements and we need new direction from God. Unusual renewal experiences with God can overcome these tendencies and redirect a leader. Openness to them, a willingness to take steps to receive them, and knowledge of their importance can be vital factors in moving towards finishing well.

Application and Discussion Questions:

1. How would you assess your learning posture? How open are you to learning and growing, as you get older?

2. As you read through the definition of renewal experiences, how many different types of these experiences have you had already?

3. How is your track record with learning 'new' things?

4. What steps are you taking to 'pass on' what God has done in you?

5. Have you experienced falling into a rut? If yes, how did you get out of it?

6. If you could 'order' a certain kind of renewal experience, what would you ask God for? Why?

Chapter 8

Focused Living for Convergence

In this chapter I (Paul) will take a look at J. Robert Clinton's (*Clinton's Biblical Leadership Commentary*) concept of "focused living." Clinton defines a focused life as:

> "A focused life is a life dedicated to exclusively carrying out God's unique purposes... by identifying the focal issues of life purpose, major role, effective methodology [and] ultimate contribution, which allows an increasing prioritization of life's activities around the focal issues, and results in a satisfying life of being [spiritual formation] and doing [leadership and strategic formation]." (p. 403)

Clinton lists four focal points in this definition. I will describe each of these in more detail and I will give you some personal examples of how I have applied them to my life and leadership over the years (as of 2012, I am 63 years old):

1. *Life Purpose* – "a burden-like calling, a task or driving force or achievement, which motivates a leader to fulfill something or to see something done" (Clinton, p. 403).

PERSONAL EXAMPLE - For me, my life purpose is "to identify, train, deploy, and support leaders (especially younger emerging leaders) for the church and the soon coming harvest (in the North American context)." This has become clearer over time and now serves as the "bull's eye" or "sweet spot" for my life and leadership.

Also, I have discovered over time that God has uniquely prepared me for this purpose through spiritual formation (Character) and leadership formation (Competencies). My gift mix and leadership experiences are the context for understanding and implementing my purpose. My primary spiritual gifts seem to be prophecy, teaching, and leadership (with secondary gifts of faith, mercy, and exhortation). I have a future orientation (prophecy), an equipping orientation (teaching), and a leadership development orientation (leadership).

Clinton has observed a general age related pattern for discovering life purpose (p. 403):

- During our 20's – commitment, character, and initial sense of purpose.

- During our 30's – leadership experience and more specific sense of purpose.

- During our 40's – clarification, modification, and expansion of major role along with deepening sense of purpose.

- During our 50's and 60's – life purpose, major role, and unique methodologies are in place resulting in effective service to others.

- During our 60's (my age) and beyond – focus is on finishing well and realizing the fulfillment of ultimate contributions (legacy).

2. *Major Role* – "is the official or unofficial position, or status/platform, or leadership functions, or job description" (Clinton, p. 403) that we function in as we try to fulfill our purpose. Major role involves base and functional components. Base components involve job position/job description and status. These components can provide a context and opportunities for leadership, but do not ensure effectiveness. Functional components involve gift mix, unique methodologies, sphere of influence, and strategic direction. These components are critical for effectiveness in leadership.

PERSONAL EXAMPLE – I served for over a dozen years as the Executive Director for Leadership Development with Open Bible Churches (base components). My function in that position was "to identify, train, deploy, and support leaders" (purpose). Over the years I helped develop five primary delivery systems to accomplish this (functional components). When I transitioned out of my formal position with Open Bible Churches a couple of years ago and established my own consulting business, the Convergence group, I changed my base components while maintaining and enlarging my functional components. I am now "identifying, training, deploying, and supporting leaders" in a larger context involving marketplace as well as ministry leaders.

According to Clinton, major role (in terms of functional components) usually begins to firm up in our 40's. Prior to this we are learning about roles that enhance or block achievement of our deepening sense of life purpose. Not all roles are equal in terms of fulfillment of life purpose. We need to find the right role if we are to be fulfilled and effective.

3. *Effective Methodologies* – "insights around which the leader can pass on to others the essentials of doing something or using something or being something, that is, a means of effectively delivering some

Starting Well

important ministry... which enhances life purpose or moves toward ultimate contribution[s]" (Clinton, p. 404).

Discovering effective methodologies is a trial and error process for most of us. We learn what does not work, what works, and what works for us as we discover and develop our gift mix (spiritual gifts, natural abilities, and acquired skills). Because a methodology works for someone else does not mean that it will work for us. We may try something that works for others and adapt (or discard) it as we evaluate "fit" in terms of our sense of life purpose, core values, and unique leadership philosophy.

PERSONAL EXAMPLE – I have developed my own unique philosophy of leadership and methodologies based on my conviction that Jesus is the primary model of Kingdom leadership. He not only demonstrated the personal character of the model Kingdom leader, but he also demonstrated the methodology for effective Kingdom leadership.

Simply put, Jesus ministered compassionately to the multitudes while investing intentionally in a few faithful followers. I call this the M>E>M (Mentoring>Empowering>Multiplication) strategy of Jesus as he empowered his disciples to "do greater works" when he departed. The application of this in my leadership is to find roles that afford me the opportunity to be exposed to younger emerging leaders who I can empower through teaching and mentoring.

Clinton points out that most leaders do not become really proficient in their unique methodologies until their 50's and beyond. Prior to this, we are usually in an "on the job training" process where we learn by trial and error and evaluation, which ultimately can lead to unique methodologies that are effective and fulfilling for us.

4. *Ultimate Contributions* – "a lasting legacy of a Christian worker for which he or she is remembered and which furthers the cause of [Christ]..." (Clinton, p. 404-405). Lasting legacy (p. 512) is described in the context of one or more of the following qualities:

- *Character* - setting standards for life and leadership.

- *Ministry {Leadership}* - impacting lives through evangelism and/or disciple-making (mentoring).

- *Catalytic* - serving as a change agent who helps make the world better.

- *Organizational* - leaving behind an organization, institution, or movement that will impact society in kingdom-advancing ways.

- *Ideation* - discovering, developing, describing, communicating, or promoting ideas that helps others come to or grow in faith.

Clinton has identified 12 ultimate contributions in his research that relate to one or more of these legacy qualities. They include (p. 512):

Character:
1. SAINT – a person who has a model life: not a perfect one, but a life others want to emulate.
2. STYLISTIC PRACTITIONER – a person who has a model ministry or organizational style that sets the pace for others and which others want to emulate.

Ministry {Leadership}:
3. MENTOR – a person who empowers others through individual or small group influence.
4. PUBLIC RHETORICIAN – a person who empowers others through effective communication to large groups.

Catalytic:
5. PIONEER – a person who starts apostolic (missionary/entrepreneurial) organizations or enterprises.
6. CHANGE PERSON – a person who is able to influence cultures to better organizations or correct social injustice in society.
7. ARTIST – a person who is able to impact organizations or cultures through innovation and creative breakthroughs.

Organizational:
8. FOUNDER – a person who establishes a new organization to meet needs or capture the essence of cultural change.
9. STABILIZER – a person who can help fledgling organizations develop and move toward stability, efficiency, and effectiveness.

Idealion:
10. RESEARCHER – a person who develops new ideas or concepts from study and research.
11. WRITER – a person who is able to conceptualize, contextualize, and communicate ideas effectively in a written format.
12. PROMOTER – a person who is able to promote new ideas through motivation or networking strategies that expand exposure and buy in.

I have given only a brief overview of ultimate contributions here to illustrate how they relate to focused living. Richard will describe ultimate contributions and their importance for finishing well in more detail in Chapter 10: Ultimate Contributions and Legacy.

PERSONAL EXAMPLE: As best I know (and it will be for others to ultimately determine this), my ultimate contributions will be mentor, writer, and promoter. I have attempted to establish, maintain, and expand my spiritual formation (Character) and exercise spiritual authority as the basis of my life and leadership influence and effectiveness.

This is the foundation on which I have established my teaching/mentoring (MENTOR) methodology for empowering leaders (especially younger leaders). From my many years of teaching and mentoring, I have developed a very large resource file of information that has become the source for my workbook series and other writing (WRITER). Also, along the way, in part because of the relationships that I have developed through mentoring, I have become networked with folks who share my paradigm for leadership development. This has lead to opportunities to connect people who are interested in this paradigm to other key people who can empower and resource them (PROMOTER).

Balance and Wholeness in Focused Living

The extraordinary power of a focused life involves the transformation of all aspects of a person's life: spiritual, physical, mental, emotional, and social. The following diagram gives a general picture of what this looks like.

Although the focus of this book (and the other two in our Well Trilogy) is the center of this diagram – LOVE, I want to make sure that I give adequate attention to the importance of balance and wholeness in the life and leadership of those who finish well. Although, I believe that we are primarily spiritual beings, I also recognize that we have to live in a material world where physical, mental, emotional, and social health and wholeness play an important part in our spiritual development and ultimate fulfillment and effectiveness in this life.

Diagram 4: The Extraordinary Power of a Focused Life

THE EXTRAORDINARY POWER OF A FOCUSED LIFE

The goal of this command is love, which comes from a pure heart and a good conscience and a sincere faith.

I Timothy 1:5

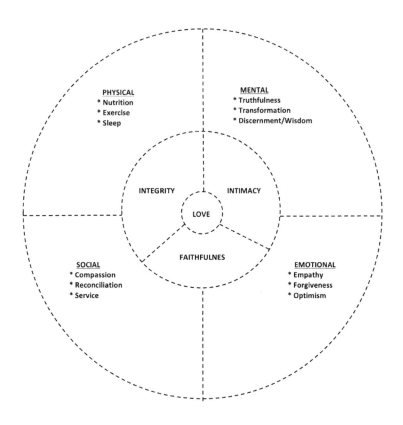

If our health is out of balance because we have neglected its proper care, we will not be able to experience life to its fullest! It is the same with our mental, emotional, and social lives! We are responsible to steward our whole being, not just our spiritual lives. Let me suggest that there are some basic components in each of these areas that we need to give attention to if we are to be the balanced and whole people God created us to be.

This is not to say that we ought to neglect our spiritual lives, which are eternal, to gratify our material lives, which are temporal. I am trying to argue here for balance and wholeness. With this in mind, let's take a look at some basic components in each of the four material areas of our life that may need attention along the way.

Disclaimer – I am not a professional or expert in any of these areas. I am not suggesting that my insights are absolute by any means. I am just trying to advocate for a context that brings all aspects of our life into balance for maximum health, wholeness, fulfillment, and effectiveness.

First, let's look at the *physical*. If we are not doing well physically, it affects everything. Good health is a blessing that we need to steward as much as we can. I have identified three components here that can help us maintain balance and wholeness in our physical lives:

- Nutrition – we need to learn to eat healthy meals to keep our weight down, blood sugar and cholesterol in healthy ranges, etc. Poor nutrition can lead to ailments that can drain and distract us from significant opportunities.

- Exercise – we need to exercise regularly to keep our cardiovascular system healthy and as a way of reducing stress. Lack of exercise can lead to sluggishness and fatigue, especially as we get older.

- Sleep – we need to get enough sleep so that we do not end up running on empty. Adequate sleep ranges vary for each individual, but getting enough rest is critical for a healthy life.

Next, let's take a look at the *mental*. Our thought life is often a picture of the rest of our life. If our thought life is balanced and wholesome, then the rest of our life and leadership will tend to be more manageable and healthy. Let me suggest three components of our mental life that we need to manage in order to be balanced and whole:

- Truthfulness – we need to learn to be people of the Word who live and speak the truth in love. Part of this involves having a clear conscience – being right with God and others as much is it is possible on our part. Being confessed up leads to a life of authenticity and transparency.

- Transformation – we need to learn how to take every thought captive to the obedience of Christ (II Corinthians 10: 5) that leads to transformation. We can learn to think and act like Jesus more and more with time.

- Discernment/Wisdom – we need to grow and mature in such a way that we become more wise and discerning about the things of God so that we can live in God's grace and be of help to others.

The third area that we will take a brief look at is the *emotional*. Learning to manage our emotional life can be challenging, whether you are the expressive type or a stuffer. There is richness about our emotional life that is part of being fully human. Let me suggest three components of our emotional life that are important for balance and wholeness:

- Empathy – we need to learn how to "feel with" others who are hurting or rejoicing. This is part of connecting with others in mature relationships of mutual benefit. Being a good listener or sharing a kind word can be a blessing to another in a timely way.

- Forgiveness – we must learn to forgive in order to be balanced, whole, and free. When we fail to forgive we become enslaved and when we forgive we become free to bless. We can never be enslaved by another or to life's circumstances if we learn how to forgive.

- Optimism – we need to see the potential for redemption in the midst of life's challenges and disappointments. We need to learn to see life in such a way that God is at work and can do the impossible to cause all things to work for good (Romans 8: 28).

This brings me to our last area, the *social*. We are social creatures. We need one another in healthy relationships to be balanced, whole, and fulfilled. Some of us are more outgoing than others, but we all need to belong and to be valued. Here are three components of our social life that we need to cultivate in order to be balanced and whole:

- Compassion – we need to value others as image bearers of God (no matter how distorted that image may be at the time). Just as Jesus had compassion on people because they were broken, lost, and hurting, so we need to learn how to express this kind of compassion to others.

- Reconciliation – we need to learn to be peacemakers and maintainers - to help reconcile broken relationships and communities. When relationships break down, we need to learn how to hear the other side of the story, to understand the estrangement of others, and then work toward bringing people together.

- Service – we need to learn how to serve like Jesus, who humbled himself in order to meet the needs of others. Service often involves sacrifice or preferring others and can be a powerful expression of the power of God to transform lives and communities.

Obviously, this is a very brief look at balance and wholeness, but it is a context that is important as we talk about focused living and what a focused life looks like. Our spiritual core is foundational for finishing well, but by neglecting any of the four natural components we can diminish the quality and ultimate impact of our lives, leadership, and legacy.

Application and Discussion Questions

1. What are the four focal points of Clinton's definition of focused living? What do you think are your characteristics related to these focal points?

2. What are ultimate contributions? Which of them is part of your sense of destiny?

3. What are the three qualities of a healthy and whole physical life? How are you doing in each of these?

4. What are the three qualities of a healthy and whole mental life? How are you doing in each of these?

5. What are the three qualities of a healthy and whole emotional life? How are you doing in each of these?

6. What are the three qualities of a healthy and whole social life? How are you doing in each of these?

7. Are there any areas that you really need to give attention to? If so, what is your plan of action and who is going to hold you accountable?

Chapter 9

Spiritual Authority

Nearly Derailed

I (Richard) will never forget that day. It was the day when all of my confidence concerning leadership using God's authority came crashing down. I can still feel the emotions surge up in me if I dial up the memories. I had just been falsely accused of something that I had not done and the accusation was being used to fire me. I was about to lose my job.

When I asked for the source of or proof of the accusation, I was told, "God has spoken to us." The very people who were confronting me were leaders who claimed to have authority from God to speak for him and I had really trusted them. I will not share all the sordid details, but it was an experience that made me ask many questions: How can God trust his leaders with his authority? How can leaders get it so wrong? Is it possible to use the authority God gives us in a way that honors God?

That day was one of the most difficult and influential days of my personal leadership development. Of course, on that day, I was just shocked, hurt, and angry. But now as I reflect back, I recognize the hand of God. He was touching me, leading me. This painful experience caused me to go deeper into the presence of God and it gave me a deep desire for learning about using authority in a way that honors God.

When a leader starts out in the ministry, the issue of authority is important. Most of our early lessons are focused on learning to submit to God's authority. Many of these lessons are learned while having to submit to leaders who have the responsibility to oversee our ministry. Many of the lessons that God teaches us are not easy to learn because of the people who are involved. We tend to focus on the people and miss God's hand. It is easy to get derailed or sidetracked when we are on the receiving side of a leader who abuses their authority. Nearly every leader I have talked with over the years can tell stories about problems with ungodly uses of authority… in the name of God.

When a leader reaches the mid-life, they will have increasing opportunities to use God's authority. Most leaders will now be in positions where they are using their authority to influence different aspects of the ministry. They make decisions about people. Which people get promoted, demoted, rewarded, punished, hired or fired? Which doors of opportunity will open or close for a potential leader? Which projects or budget requests get approved or denied? As a preacher, teacher, mentor, evangelist, coach, prophetic voice or boss, a leader will on a regular basis represent God and speak for him.

The lessons concerning authority in the middle stages are centered on learning to use our authority in a way that honors God. Will we focus in on leaders who are modeling Godly uses of authority and learn from them? Will we repeat the mistakes of leaders who have gone before us? Will we develop healthy patterns of using authority or will we fall into abusive patterns?

The abuse of authority is one of the traps that cause leaders to crash out in leadership. Leaders are in greatest danger of falling into this trap in the middle stages of leadership. There are many issues in a leader's life that make them vulnerable to abusing authority such as ambition, insecurity, feeling threatened, unresolved hurts, and lack of forgiveness.

In the end game, leaders will be in ministry roles and positions where their influence and authority are usually the greatest. Some will be heavily involved in direct ministry roles where their use of authority and influence are directly influencing people under them. Many will be in roles of indirect ministry where their influence and use of authority is more behind the scenes. Their use of authority and influence are not as visible, but they are the leaders who are pulling the strings. They are involved in the decisions that have ramifications throughout the ministry settings they are involved in.

In the end game, leaders have to pay special care and attention to the way they use their authority and influence. For these reasons, I think it is important to review what the Bible reveals to us about a God honoring use of authority. My prayer is that this chapter will help us go deeper into God's presence so that we can learn to use his authority in a way that brings glory to him.

Spiritual Authority: Commissioned by God

In Luke 9, we are told that one day Jesus gathered his band of disciples together. They had been with him for some time and had watched how he lived his life and interacted with others. They had listened to and learned from him. I do not know what the disciples were expecting when Jesus gathered them together on that day, but I imagine the last thing that they expected was for Jesus to say, "I give you my authority. Break up into teams of two and go from village to village and do what you have seen me doing. I will check in with you later" (Matthew 10: 1, Clinton paraphrase).

I imagine there was a gasp of surprise in heaven from all the angels watching. The great cloud of witnesses gathered around the throne watching might have even let out a little groan. I imagine a few eyebrows were raised by some of the saints from the Old Testament gathered around the throne.

It is hard to say how the disciples felt as they scattered and walked towards the villages in the distance. I imagine they were pretty nervous and maybe a little uncertain. They were to announce the good news about the Kingdom of God and were to drive out demons and heal the sick. They were to do what they had seen Jesus do.

I am sure that they had many questions, but I think one thing was very clear to them - they were not going to do this in their own strength. They were not doing this in their own names. They were representing Jesus, the Messiah. They knew it was his authority and were using it to preach good news about the kingdom, drive out the demons, and heal the sick.

In Luke 10, Jesus selected another group of disciples and sent them out to do the same thing. And they did it! When they came back to Jesus, they were filled with surprise and joy. It worked! That is probably what I would have shouted. It was very clear to them that they did not do any of this in their own power, own ability, or own authority. They went in the name of Jesus and acted in his authority.

In Matthew 28, Jesus extends the same commission to all disciples who will follow him. In this passage, Jesus made sure that we know that we must function in his authority if we want to accomplish his will. All authority for leadership in the Kingdom of God belongs to the King. Anyone who uses authority in his kingdom is doing so by using his authority. In every situation where we talk about authority and the use of authority, we must begin with this point. It is not our authority, but the Kings.

Imagining myself being in the same situation as those disciples really helps me. I wonder how I would have done in that situation. After all, many people would have already heard something about Jesus. They had heard about his signs and wonders and would have had some expectations about Jesus. They would have wanted to see if what they had heard about Jesus was true or not. Then I try to imagine myself walking with Jesus from village to village and exercising the authority that he had given me.

And, should it be any different when I walk into my church or any ministry setting to announce the good news about Jesus, announce that his kingdom is near, drive out the demons, heal the sick, select small group leaders, make a budget for the ministry, decide which projects get a thumbs up or a thumbs down, offer a word of counsel, solve the problems that arise when people work together or solve the problems that come against what God wants to do with us? It is all the business of the King.

Leadership and Authority

Leaders need authority to lead. This is a simple fact. If a leader does not have any authority, it is impossible to lead. Society makes this point abundantly clear. We observe what happens when people reject authority. When students reject or don't accept the authority of a teacher, what chance does a teacher have of leading those students? It is true in every place where leaders are trying to lead followers. Authority is a critical issue for effective leadership.

What is authority? The simplest definition I can think of is that authority is the right to use power. What is power? It is the ability, force, or energy used to accomplish something. It has been defined as "a capacity to control or influence others."

Leadership is using this capacity to produce a specific response from the followers. Dennis Wrong adapts Bertrand Russell's definition of power and defines power as "the capacity of some person to produce intended and foreseen effects on others" (*Power*, p. 2). Leaders need authority to lead. Without authority, there is no way to use power to do something. Power is what gets a task accomplished.

But the question is: Where does a leader get their authority? There are many different sources of authority. There are many different ways that a leader uses power to get the followers to do what they want.

I believe that effective leaders in the Kingdom of God understand the use of authority and learn to operate with spiritual authority as their primary means of using power. Christian leaders can legitimately use other sources of authority, but I believe that God challenges us through the numerous models of leadership recorded in the Bible to increasingly use spiritual authority as the primary means of influencing the followers God has given us. It is the primary source of leadership authority that Jesus used. And he calls us to follow his example and use his authority in the same way that he did.

To truly understand what spiritual authority is all about, we need to understand something about authority. What are the different sources a leader draws on to gain authority and what are the various means of using power?

Dennis Wrong's Categories of Leadership Power

Dennis Wrong's book *Power* is very helpful in understanding the various forms of power that leaders use. He examines the means by which a leader gains influence with followers and how a leader gains the compliance of the followers. In simpler language, he points out the ways that a leader gets the followers to do what the leader wants. Wrong identifies the dynamics that are involved in this use of power. Using power must be based on the acceptance of authority. He points out that there are various sources of authority.

Spiritual Authority

His categories and definitions are helpful for arriving at an understanding of what spiritual authority is and how it functions.

1. **The Use of Force** - One means to get the followers to do what the leader wants is to use force. Force, either physical or psychological, can be used to get the followers to do what the leader wants. The source of authority lies in greater weapons, the might of an army, or greater control over information or the flow of information. The follower does not have a choice about whether they do what the leader wants or not. The leader who controls the power makes the followers comply. This does not mean that the force is always bad. For example, police officers need to use force at times. There are times when parents need to use force to protect their children. When a child steps toward a busy street, a powerful restraining hand is needed.

2. **The Use of Manipulation** - Manipulation refers to the situation where a leader gains compliance of a follower and where the follower does not have awareness of the leader's intents. Therefore, the follower does not necessarily have the freedom to exert moral responsibility in the situation. The followers are making the choice about whether to follow the leader or not, but they do not necessarily have all the information or understanding of the situation. Manipulation in our day is seen as bad. Since the days of the Enlightenment, individuals have believed that we have the right to know all the facts and understand them for ourselves. All manipulation violates this understanding and, thus, is bad.

    But there can be legitimate uses of manipulation in situations where the leader has good motives or intentions for not revealing everything to the follower. An example of this was when Jesus manipulated his disciples into becoming "fishers of men." He asked them to leave everything behind and follow him before they really understood what that meant. At that time, they could not comprehend the motivation and intention of Jesus. If Jesus had told them everything about what it meant to follow him, how would they have responded? I for one am glad that God did not tell me everything that I would encounter in following him. I prefer trusting him and following him one step at a time.

3. **The Use of Persuasion** - Persuasion refers to a situation where a leader uses things such as arguments, appeals, or exhortations to gain the compliance of the follower and yet protects the freedom of the follower to exercise moral responsibility. A leader lays everything out on the table and asks the follower to evaluate it and make a choice. This is the form of power that we respond to the easiest in the Western world.

4. **The Use of Coercion** - The use of coercion is another way that a leader gets the followers to do what the leader wants. It involves the leader using the threat of force or threat of punishment. Do such and such or else! Leaders can induce followers to obey by using the promise of a reward where the follower is gaining something valuable.

Position, Role, Competency, Personality, and Authority

Certain positions or roles carry a legitimate authority. The boss of a company or being a parent or a teacher brings a certain amount of authority. The leader can use this authority to get the follower to do what they want as long as what they are asking for falls within the expected use of that authority. For example, a boss can ask for work related things but when they ask for compliance outside of the work environment they run into problems. Both the leader and follower need to have the same expectation concerning the authority that comes with the position.

There is a certain amount of authority that comes with being competent in an area. Followers recognize that competency and allow the leader to influence them. For example, a pro-golfer that is giving beginners a few tips. The golf pro can expect that the beginners would follow his advice, but cannot demand it. The beginners are free to choose if they want to follow or not. And the golf pro and his authority are limited to his area of expertise and their openness to his influence.

Sometimes a person gains authority over others by virtue of their personal characteristics. This is often attributed to the personal charisma or the magnetism of the leader's personality. This person can expect followers (admirers) to comply with their requests, but cannot demand it. Followers accept their leadership authority and allow themselves to be influenced by that leader. Famous media personalities often utilize this kind of authority in order to get followers to accept their influence. This is the whole idea behind many marketing campaigns.

There are several types of power (force, persuasion, manipulation, and coercion) that interact with issues like position, role, competency, and personality to contextualize authority and its influence on followers. With this foundational understanding of leadership, power and authority, we can now define spiritual authority.

What is Spiritual Authority?

J.R. Clinton defines spiritual authority as "the right to influence followers that is conferred upon a leader by followers because of their perception of spirituality in that leader's life." This definition could fit every spiritual leader in every religion in the world. In the Christian context, I would define spiritual authority like this, "Spiritual authority is the right to use power and authority that is given to the leader because the followers recognize the presence of God operating in the life of the leader."

Pay close attention! Spiritual authority is given to the leader by the followers. Maybe a better way to say it is this, "Followers will recognize that God has worked in the leader's life in such a way that they accept God's authority being in the leader and allow the leader to lead them on this basis." In this sense, God gives spiritual authority. To use Jesus as an example of this - Jesus demonstrated the authority of God, but his followers had to recognize it in him.

The leader cannot just stand up and say, "God has given me his authority! Obey me!" Although I have seen many Christian leaders try this. I have received my seminary degree... now I am a spiritual leader! Followers do not automatically give the right to use power because of a theological degree.

There is another feature of spiritual authority that is important. A leader cannot demand obedience from the followers on the basis of spiritual authority. Operating in spiritual authority by definition means that the followers are free to choose whether or not they want to obey. Is not this what God does with every human being? God does not force us to obey him. He allows us to choose. Therefore, it makes sense that leaders who are using God's authority would operate in the same way.

A person operating in spiritual authority does not necessarily have a role, position, or title that gives them the right to use power in this way. Spiritual authority does not come with the job description. It comes from the followers who recognize it in the leader. Certain roles, positions, or titles create other sources of authority, but may not involve spiritual authority. Spiritual authority comes when the followers recognize the presence of God in the leader's life and they allow them to exert influence.

How Does God Give His Authority to a Leader?

If God gives his authority to us, how does he do it? Is it a process or does it happen from one moment to the next? I believe that the answer is both! God gives his authority in moments where we surrender our lives to him and he calls us to serve him as a leader. The Holy Spirit fills us with his presence and we are "authorized" to be leaders for the Kingdom of God.

Jesus called his disciples to himself and gave them authority. This happened from one moment to the next. It was an event and when they went from village to village and used that authority, people who were on the receiving end of their being "authorized" would have recognized God's presence. At the moment they announced that the Kingdom of God was near healing and deliverance happened. It was the demonstration of power that went together with their words that provided the evidence in the perception of these villagers that God's presence was with them.

The Capacity to Use Spiritual Authority

At the same time, it is a process. God works into our lives the capacity to function with spiritual authority. There is a process that we see God using throughout the stories of his leaders in the Bible. In our (my father and I) leadership studies, we have discerned three primary ways that God builds the capacity for using spiritual authority.

1. *God takes us through what we call "deep processing".* In these experiences, God transforms us and the evidence is visible for others to see. "Deep processing" simply means the pressure filled times, the difficult times, the testing times and the crisis times. They can be experiences that occur because of circumstances outside of the control of the leader or can be experiences that happen completely on the inside of person... invisible to anyone else. They can be

circumstances that come about because of poor choices made by the leader or they can occur because of choices made by someone else. There is no rule for how these experiences begin. However, when they start the leader goes through a deep and difficult time (for more information about this see Chapter 6: Deep Processing).

As leaders go through deep experiences with God, they experience the sufficiency of God to meet them in those situations and come to know God in deeper and more intimate ways. They draw near to God and God draws near to them. This closeness to God under pressure is visible to followers. Followers then allow the leader to operate with spiritual authority.

In the New Testament, the Apostle Paul exemplifies this nearness to God during deep, pressure packed, and difficult situations. A major part of Paul's defense of his apostolic authority (II Corinthians) is based on the numerous and wide variety of difficult, painful experiences that he had gone through. He listed them as a part of his defense and talked about suffering, disappointments, and crushing pressure he had endured. It was clear that his defense rested on the fact that even though all these things happened, the presence of God was visible in his life. He essentially said, "You know me, what I have been through, and how God has proven himself powerful in my weakness."

A leader is revealed for who he really is during times of pressure. What lies deep on the inside will come out during deep processing. God touches the person at the deepest levels and who he is becomes visible to the people around. In II Corinthians 1: 3-4, Paul revealed that one of benefits of deep processing was to get closer to God. He wanted to encounter the God of all comfort and receive comfort that he could in turn pass it along to others who needed it.

What happens to a leader who goes through deep processing is one of the critical aspects of running well, fighting well, and remaining faithful (II Timothy 4: 7). The choices that a leader makes will determine whether he or she allows the pressure to push them deeper into God's presence or push them away from God.

Every one of us chooses which way we will turn. The leaders who turn into God grow in their capacity to use spiritual authority.

2. *The life transforming process that we call sanctification is another way that God builds the capacity for spiritual authority.* God forms us into the image of Christ. Paul wrote about this in Romans 8: 28-30 when he said:

> "And we know that all things work together for good to them that love God, to them who are the called according to His purpose, for whom He did foreknow, He also did predestinate to be conformed to the image of His Son, that He might be the premiere exemplar among many followers. Moreover whom He did predestinate, them He also called; and whom He called, them He also justified and whom He justified, them He also glorified."

In Colossians 1: 27-29, he wrote:

> "To them God has chosen to make known among the Gentiles the glorious riches of this mystery, which is Christ in you, the hope of glory. We proclaim Him, admonishing and teaching everyone with all wisdom, so that we may present everyone perfect in Christ. To this end I labor struggling in intercession with all His energy which so powerfully works in me."

In Galatians 4: 19, he wrote:

> "My little children, of whom I travail in birth again until Christ be formed in you."

In Galatians 5, Paul lists a number of qualities that the Holy Spirit is working into our life. He calls them the fruit of the Holy Spirit: love, joy, peace, patience, gentleness, goodness, faithfulness, gentleness and self-control. When followers discern these qualities in a leader's life, they carry great weight and give the leader credibility. It is the presence of these Godly character qualities that are visible to followers. This is especially true when these characteristics are seen under pressure.

Daniel (Daniel 6) is one of those characters in the Bible who really exemplified a strong God honoring character. His integrity and allegiance to God was well known to everyone. Even his enemies counted on Daniel to maintain his integrity. If Daniel had wavered, their plan to trap him and kill him would not have worked. His hunger for truth and his desire to be close to his God was well know. And it was lived out under the most difficult of circumstances. Followers see the presence of God in our lives when they discern Godly character. This recognition creates the capacity for a leader to use spiritual authority to influence followers in Godly ways.

3. *A third way that God creates the capacity for using spiritual authority is to release his power through a leader.* We call this operating in gifted power. God releases the power of the Holy Spirit when we use the spiritual gifts that he has given us. The effect of those gifts and the tangible power of God are recognizable to the followers. This demonstrates in a clear way that God's presence is with the leader. This gives them credibility and allows them to use spiritual authority.

God can use any of the spiritual gifts, but this effect is especially seen when God uses the gifts (i.e. miraculous gifts) where it is clearly God's power at work. There are many examples of God using leaders in this way. Besides Jesus, Moses was one of those leaders who powerfully demonstrated this in the ten plagues (see Exodus 7-11).

God's power that was released through Moses towards Pharoah and the Egyptians as God set his people free from slavery was incredible. The miracle of the parting of the Red Sea when God delivered the people of Israel from the Egyptian army was almost unbelievable. Moses' encounter with God on the mountain changed the way that the people of Israel saw him. And there were many other examples of God's presence with him. God confirmed his authority in Moses through miraculous signs and wonders. None of the Israelites ever questioned the presence of God and his connection to Moses. They questioned other things... all the time, but God's presence with Moses was in evidence every day. God's power moving through Moses created the capacity to use spiritual authority as he led God's people.

Most of us can't relate to the story of Moses and these kinds of demonstrations of power, but we do know what it is like when God fills a leader with his power and uses that leader to do something that was clearly beyond their capacity. I have experienced this on several occasions. God used people in ways that clearly demonstrated that God was directing them or using them to touch my life or to give me a message from God. In each one of those situations, I recognized God's presence in the person's life and allowed them to influence me. I allowed them to use spiritual authority to lead me.

I have also been on the other side of the story on some occasions when God used me in ways that clearly demonstrated his presence and his power. I have always been deeply stirred when I read what Paul said to the church in Corinth, "My message and my preaching were not with wise and persuasive words, but with a demonstration of the Spirit's power, so that your faith might not rest on men's wisdom, but on God's power" (I Corinthians 2: 4-5).

Two Things We Should Do

I believe that God wants to reveal himself to people and one of the clearest ways to do that is to release his Spirit's power through his leaders. This is such an important part of being a spiritual leader especially in the end game when we have the opportunity to model the way and impart what we have learned along the way to others. Here are a couple of guidelines for functioning in spiritual authority during the end game:

1. **Seek God** - God works into our lives the capacity to function with spiritual authority. There is a process that we see God using throughout the stories of his leaders in the Bible. It is not the goal of a leader to gain spiritual authority, but to use spiritual authority as their primary means for influencing others. It is the means, not the goal. Spiritual authority is a byproduct of being close to God.

A leader does not seek to get spiritual authority. A leader seeks to know God. As a leader experiences God, spiritual authority is a byproduct. We seek God through the deep, intense experiences of life. As we encounter him in these times, we are changed. God's presence becomes more visible. We seek God and ask for his transforming, sanctifying presence. We seek to become like Christ in our character and followers will recognize God's presence in our lives. We seek to be open and obedient to allow God to use us to bring his presence, his word, and his touch to the lives of people around us. When we do this, his power flows through us. These transforming experiences create the capacity to use spiritual authority with our followers.

2. **Seek to Become Mature** - I would like to finish this chapter by looking at a leader who learned to use spiritual authority in a mature way. His model and his example speak to us today. In recent years, so many leadership problems have arisen in ministry because of the misuse of authority by leaders. Following the model that we see in this leader will help us to avoid many of the problems that cause leaders to fail. We can learn much from this story.

The story I am referring to is what happened to the Apostle Paul and his relationship to the people in the church in Corinth. This story is communicated to us in the book of II Corinthians. Paul's leadership is being attacked and he defended his authority to act as a leader in this troubled church. He defended his calling as an Apostle and his right to use apostolic authority.

Apostolic authority was not tied to a position of leadership in the early church. Paul had planted the church in Corinth and was the main spiritual leader who influenced the early development of this church. He had established the leadership in the church, but he had no positional authority there. Paul's influence and use of authority was made on the basis of spiritual authority.

His method of defense and his style of leadership revealed some critical points about using spiritual authority. There are many points that could be made, but I want to focus in on five of them. He defended his authority and his leadership by pointing to his motives and how his actions revealed his motives.

Five Lessons About Paul's Motives for Using Authority

1. *A leader using spiritual authority is motivated by a deep love and concern for the followers.* Here is how Paul expressed this to the people in the church at Corinth:

* If we suffer…it is for you. If we are comforted…it is for you. (II Corinthians 1: 6)
* I want you to know that my love for you motivates my actions. (II Corinthians 2: 4)
* We operate in a transparent way. We don't preach ourselves but Christ. We are simply slaves of Jesus. We are pressured, attacked, crushed and we carry a burden for your benefit. (II Corinthians 4: 1-18)
* Everything we do dear friends is for your strengthening. (II Corinthians 12: 19)

2. *A leader using spiritual authority is not motivated by personal needs, personal concerns or personal desires.* Again, let's hear from Paul's own words:

* We don't promote ourselves. Christ's love for the Corinthian believers compels our actions. (II Corinthians 12: 19)
* We did not do ministry for money. We supported ourselves. My love for you motivates my actions with you. (II Corinthians 11: 7-12)

3. *A leader using spiritual authority does things in open, honest, and transparent ways.* Paul defended his integrity in the following way:

* We have acted as leaders with a clear conscious, holiness, and sincerity. (II Corinthians 1:12)
* We have wronged no one, corrupted no one, exploited no one and we don't condemn anyone. (II Corinthians 7:2-3)

4. *A leader using spiritual authority is not heavy handed or demanding. Spiritual authority is demonstrated in cooperation and service.* Again, in Paul's own words:

* I didn't use my authority to "lord it over you". We work with you. (II Corinthians 1:24)
* With meekness and gentleness I defend my authority. I was given authority for building you up not pulling you down. Authority has limits set by God. (II Corinthians 10: 1-18)
* This is why I am writing this to you. I want to use the authority that the Lord gave me for building you up and not tearing you down. (II Corinthians 13:10)

5. *A leader using spiritual authority points followers to God and is aware that their leadership is under him.* Paul, again, defended his right to lead via spiritual authority:

* We don't want to block anyone from God. We have endured great difficulties. We have operated with a godly character, purity, understanding, patience and kindness, truthful speech. We did this freely so that you could receive freely. (II Corinthians 6:3-13)

Paul demonstrates in this defense of his leadership that the main issue related to the proper use of authority is motivation. What is the motivation of the leader? Our motives are very important. Leaders who are using spiritual authority are motivated by the love that Jesus has for the followers. They are willing to sacrifice themselves and to endure great suffering themselves if it means that the followers will be built up.

This is the kind of Christian leader that we need today. This is the kind of leadership motivation that more leaders should have. It is the opposite of what is going on all around us in leadership. It goes against the whole "what is in it for me" motivation. It goes against the whole power hungry, control orientation that dominates so much of leadership today.

Spiritual authority is the right to influence conferred upon a leader by followers, because of their perception of spirituality in that leader. To run well, to fight well, to remain faithful, we need more of Christ in us and less of ourselves (John 3:30). To finish well in leadership, we need to learn to lead his way and we need to become leaders who model what it means to be filled with God's presence and who use that to build up everyone else.

Application and Discussion Questions:

1. Why are the issues of authority and spiritual authority so important in the end game?

2. What abuses of authority have you seen in leadership and how has it affected the ministry setting?

3. Why does J. Robert Clinton believe that Christian leaders should move towards using spiritual authority as a primary means of using power?

4. When you reflect on your own development, what situations or what relationships has God used to develop your capacity for operating in spiritual authority?

5. What 'traps' or pitfalls lurk in the end game in regards to the issue of using authority?

   (Possible examples: relying of past experiences too much, temptation to cut a few corners, temptation to 'enjoy' privileges of a long ministry tenure, etc.)

6. In the area of using spiritual authority, what can be done to ensure a good finish and make sure the use of authority is God honoring and directs glory to God?

Chapter 10

Ultimate Contributions and Legacy

What Will the End Be Like?

In the last several years, there have been a number of films that focus on end of life issues. Films like "An Unfinished Life" and "The Bucket List" have drawn attention in a fresh way to what happens to people as they face the end of life. This is not a new thing as over the years many films and books have been made and written on this topic. There is something about the end of life and the huge question of what happens after life that attracts attention in every generation. As questions about the end draws near, many questions about the meaning of life surface in every generation. What makes life worth living? What gives meaning to life? How do I evaluate my own life?

One film that caught my (Richard) attention was a film made in 2002 called "About Schmidt." It is a meaning of life story about how our lives impact or do not impact our world. The story is sad because the main character comes face to face with a largely insignificant and meaningless existence. I think everyone who watched this film and interacted with this story asked themselves questions like:

* How am I doing?
* How is my life different from Schmidt's life?
* How is my life the same as Schmidt's life?

It is towards the end of life that most of us start to focus on how our lives have impacted the world around us. We focus in on questions like: "Has my life made any difference in the world around me?" "Has my life made a positive contribution?" I remember watching the movie and having an overwhelming emotional response - I want my life to count. I do not want to end anywhere close to where Schmidt ends up.

Living a Life That Counts: Ultimate Contributions

As followers of Jesus, we believe and know that accomplishing the purposes that God designed us for will bring an incredible sense of a satisfaction, worth, and fulfillment in life. We gave ourselves to the King and his cause. Finishing well makes life worth living.

One aspect of finishing well that I will focus on in this chapter is what we call Ultimate Contributions. When we have lived a life focused on following God, it has an impact. The impact that we leave behind; the things that we are remembered for are our ultimate contributions. It is the legacy that we leave behind. Our legacy points others in the direction of what gave our life meaning.

Many years ago, my father (J. Robert Clinton) spent some time gathering material and insights about how leaders are remembered.

He read through a series of articles published in the *International Bulletin of Missionary Research* that were dedicated to remembering the achievements of leaders. He also gathered what he called legacy material from scores of biographies written about Christian leaders. With all of these sources, he began to develop the concept of an "ultimate contribution." He began to define and categorize what he was seeing in his research.

He wrote about his findings in an article entitled, "Ultimate Contributions: A Life that Counts." What I am sharing here comes out of his research findings. He defines the concept of ultimate contribution "as a lasting legacy of a Christian worker for which he/she is remembered and which furthers the cause of Christianity by one or more of the following:

- Setting standards for life and ministry,

- Impacting lives by enfolding them in God's kingdom or developing them once in the kingdom,

- Serving as a stimulus for change which betters the world,

- Leaving behind an organization, institution, or movement that can serve as a channel for God to work through, or

- The discovery of ideas, communication of them, or promotion of them so that they further God's work. "

Clinton's Ultimate Contribution Category's and Types

As he sifted through all the data, he began to organize it into 5 categories of ultimate contributions and what he called 13 prime types of ultimate contributions. He saw that leaders often had 2 or 3 types of ultimate contributions that described the legacy that they were leaving behind. The language that he used to describe the categories and types can be a bit overwhelming so I will try to explain them as best as I can.

Category 1: Character (ultimate contributions that are focused on around the life and character of the leader):

Type 1: Saint - This type of ultimate contribution is all about a leader who lives a model life. That is, a life that others want to emulate. It doesn't mean a perfect life. The leader lives the kind of life that others want to pattern their own lives after. Usually, the person is thought of as having a very intimate, close personal connection or relationship with God. They are often leaders who have numerous mystical experiences or deep experiences with God. This closeness to God is clearly evident in the fruit of their life. The way that they interact with others demonstrates the fruit of the Holy Spirit. They live with zeal, passion, and hunger for God. The contribution that this kind of leader makes is the impact they have on others as they model this kind of life.

Type 2: Stylistic Practitioner - This type of ultimate contribution is focused on a leader who develops a style of doing ministry that becomes a model for others. Other leaders in similar ministries often copy and try to use this ministry style. Usually there is a leader who tries some ministry model that turns into a breakthrough in some and then it gets passed on and multiplied. In the age of technology that we now live in, passing things on is easier and easier. Websites, blogs, conferences, and materials are some of the ways that ministry models are spreading quickly throughout the world.

Type 3: Family - This type of ultimate contribution focuses on the leader and their family. They make choices within the context of ministry to work hard to build and nurture a God-fearing family. The relationship emphasis is especially clear in the marriage relationship and in the way that parenting is done. The goal is to lead the family in such a way that the legacy that is left behind is a pattern of relationships that show the importance of honoring God in the family. Leaving behind children who walk with God is a powerful legacy.

Category 2: Ministry (ultimate contributions that are focused on the ministry activity of a leader):

Type 4: Mentoring - This type of ultimate contribution is focused on ministry that is centered on empowering people. It describes a lifetime of productive ministry with individuals or even small groups of people. A mentor is a person whose primary impact is on individuals. Ministry is done primarily at a personal level. They develop relationships with people and focus there. Every ministry deals with people, but the person making this kind of contribution is focused on personal relationships and helping people realize their God-given potential. The people that are developed and helped are the ultimate contribution.

Type 5: Public Rhetorician - This type of ultimate contribution focuses on speaking, communication, teaching or preaching. The leader who has this type of contribution leaves behind a legacy of messages and people impacted by those messages. God uses them to speak to groups of people. Most public rhetoricians are remembered for speaking to large groups of people. Many people remember being stirred, encouraged, challenged, or provoked through their messages. This type of ultimate contribution can be found in pastoral ministry, evangelistic meetings, or motivational speaking inside or outside of the church. The lives changed through their speaking are their ultimate contribution.

Category 3: Catalytic (ultimate contributions that are focused on legacies in which new things are created or produced):

Type 6: Pioneer - This type of ultimate contribution describes a person who God uses to start new things. Leaders leaving behind this kind of legacy have the ability to see ministry that needs to be done and are able to catalyze people to meet that need. They find ways to break new ground. Sometimes the thing they are pioneering ends up launching new ministry structures, new organizations, or new churches. The ministry that is pioneered and launched is the ultimate contribution that is left behind.

Type 7: Person of Change - This type of ultimate contribution describes a person who is committed to bringing about social change. Often, they are people who commit themselves to righting wrongs and working to correct injustices in society. They can also be people who are committed to change in the context of organizations such as churches, mission agencies, and other ministry structures. They see problems and set about to bring changes that will correct the things that they see are wrong. They are remembered for the changes that were brought about and often the sacrifices that they made to bring in those changes.

Type 8: Artist - This type of ultimate contribution focuses on creative people who use their creativity to get people to respond. Artists bring creative breakthroughs to life and ministry by introducing innovation. This type of person introduces new products of various kinds into the Christian sub-culture as well as the larger culture. It may be through forms of art, new music, a new genre of writing, or some other innovative activity. Frequently, people leaving this kind of contribution have brilliant natural talents. The artistic product–hymn, new genre of writing, poetry, painting, drama, dance, or whatever is the contribution that is left behind.

<u>**Category 4: Organizational**</u> (ultimate contributions that are focused on building up and strengthening organizations.):

Ultimate Contributions and Legacy

Type 9: Founder - This type of ultimate contribution is all about starting a new organization. This ultimate contribution type is closely related to the pioneer. Often, God uses the same person to pioneer and found a new organization. The focus here is on the creation of a new organization. It is started in response to some felt need or to help capture and perpetuate something that God is doing. This person may not be able to stabilize the organization. Their role is centered on the pioneering phase and establishing the organization. Others may need to stabilize what the founder has established. The new organization and its impact on people is the ultimate contribution of the founder.

Type 10: Stabilizer - This type of ultimate contribution recognizes the value of a person who steps in alongside or shortly after a pioneer or founder launches a new organization. They provide leadership and direction that helps the fledgling organization develop. They often help lay systems or foundations that allow the organization to move forward toward efficiency and effectiveness. In other words, they help solidify an organization so that it will survive and become an on-going institution. The organization and its on-going impact on people is the ultimate contribution of the stabilizer.

<u>Category 5: Ideation</u> (ultimate contributions that are focused on discovering new ideas, communicating them and spreading them):

Type 11: Researcher - This type of ultimate contribution centers on people who can research, discern, and organize data into helpful ways so that others can understand it. This type of leader develops new ideation by study, research, and conceptualization. This is a person who sees a situation, seeks to understand it, and comes up with a framework for understanding it. This framework is usually considered a break through which aids others to see truth and its application more clearly. Their research can focus on contemporary issues and their application or fundamental dynamics

that are more timeless in their application. The basic thrust of the contribution is conceptualization.

Type 12: Writer - This type of ultimate contribution describes people who can capture ideas and reproduce them in written format to help inform others. This is a person who produces a body of literature that affects a significant group of people for a limited or timeless way in which it is continually read by generations to come. Sometimes one single work, a book, a tract, a sermon, or an article, becomes significant enough that it lives on as an ultimate contribution. The basic thrust of the contribution is the written product.

Type 13: Promoter - This type of ultimate contribution focuses on people who can effectively distributes new ideas, materials, ministry models, or other things like this to people. This type of person may or may not have originated whatever it is that they are promoting, but they are adept at marketing it and spreading the word about it. The contribution they make is the widespread acceptance and use of whatever it is that they are promoting.

The Nature of Ultimate Contributions

My father went on in his analysis of ultimate contributions and noticed several other key elements about them. He noticed that some of the contributions lasted only a short time while others lasted a long time (in our perception). Of course, God sees every contribution as being significant and they all have eternal benefits. All contributions are significant from God's perspective, but from our perspective some are more noticeable than others.

In terms of the duration or the lasting effect of some ultimate contributions, he noticed that some contributions were focused on people and are focused on the specific time or context in which they lived. He called these "contemporary" contributions. We use the

Ultimate Contributions and Legacy

category of "classic" to describe contributions that lasted beyond the lifetime of the leader and are still having impact in generations after they are gone.

The reason that this is helpful is that when we think about or evaluate what our contribution will be, we need to recognize that God rises up leaders for special situations, times, and people. Some leaders will make contemporary contributions and may not be remembered in the same way as those who make classic contributions. Both kinds of contributions are needed and God places value on both of them. We need to be careful not to use the concept of ultimate contributions as another way of evaluating and judging leaders. God values all types of contributions. Even so, for leaders who recognize that some of their contributions might be classic, they should think about investing in capturing their contribution in a form that will outlive them.

Another thing that my dad noticed is that some contributions are easily visible to others while other contributions are not easily visible. Some contributions are products, ministry structures, or organizations that can be seen easily by others. Other contributions involve processes with people that are not so readily perceived. The nature of the contribution can be a tangible product such as a book, or a theory, or an organization, or a changed institution, or it may be an intangible product such as a model life or unknown numbers of people that came to know God or were inspired in their walk with God. It is important to recognize that God sees and counts it all.

The other factor that he observed was that different leaders influence or impact varying numbers of followers. Some leaders influence great masses of people while others are focused on a few. In the Kingdom of God, we know that God determines this and establishes each person's potential to influence. As we evaluate and move towards identifying our ultimate contributions, we need to remember not to compare ourselves to others. Each one of us is on a unique journey and will have a unique legacy.

Why Concern Ourselves with Ultimate Contributions?

Some people might raise this question, Why worry about ultimate contributions? What will be will be. These folks would resist trying to figure it out and advocate letting God sort out the results of their ministry.

Other people might raise another question, Is it possible that focusing on or talking about one's ultimate contribution could lead to egotistical or self-serving approaches to ministry? I think that this is a real danger, but humility breaks the power of pride. At the same time, the danger that this presents is already present and has to be dealt with in ministry. Wrongful pride is one of the major barriers that blocks leaders from finishing well. I would suggest that if we are aware of the danger, we must take steps to avoid wrongful pride. In fact, I would suggest that our finish would be greatly enhanced by knowing something about ultimate contributions.

One of the guiding mandates in our research on understanding how God develops leaders comes out of Hebrews 13:7-8. We paraphrase it like this:

> "Remember your former leaders. Imitate those qualities and achievements that were God-honoring, for the source of their leadership still lives—Jesus. He, too, can inspire and enable your own leadership today." (Hebrews 13:7,8 Clinton paraphrase)

God wants us to think back on, reflect on, and learn from those who have gone before us. The lessons that we learn can greatly enhance our effectiveness as leaders. This is especially true for leaders who want to finish well. It is worth exploring the possible end results of our lives and to focus on making decisions along the way that show that we are cooperating with God's plans and purposes in our lives.

By understanding and gaining perspective about how God has used leaders to make specific kinds of contributions to the king-

Ultimate Contributions and Legacy

dom, we can gain valuable perspective on what God is doing in our own lives. We can make better choices along the way that can lead us towards accomplishing God's plan for our lives. The end result will be leaving behind a legacy which points to God's goodness and God's mercy.

There are several principles that lay a foundation for our work in trying to understand leadership development. My father has said it like this, "Effective leaders view their ministry in terms of a lifetime perspective. An informed perspective includes knowledge about ultimate contributions. Such knowledge increases the likelihood of a leader finishing well. A life that counts is the ultimate contribution."

The real value of doing this kind of study and evaluation in your life is especially important as leaders are moving into the end game. This transition time is a time when decisions need to be made that will help focus a leader on doing exactly what God wants them to do. Or to say it in different words, we make decisions that will allow us to live out our lives exactly as God has designed us.

Learning about the concept of ultimate contributions adds another dynamic to our lives as well. There is a suggestive power involved in evaluating our lives that helps us focus in a way that enhances the possibility of finishing well. I do not know about any of you, but there are a number of things on my "to do list" that tend to get put off as I get caught up in the day-to-day grind. I know that a number of these projects are related to my ultimate contributions.

Knowing where you are going and having the right priorities can enhance your chances of finishing well and leaving a lasting legacy. Re-orienting and re-prioritizing the way I allocate my time and energy is necessary in order for me to tackle some of these projects. The focus that comes from understanding what God is doing with me helps me to make decisions that will lead me toward accomplishing his plan for my life.

In addition to this, there are times when thinking about our future and our ultimate contributions can help us mold the ministry role that we have so that we are moving more deliberately toward what God wants to do in and through our lives. We may be able to delegate secondary responsibilities, hire to our weaknesses, or negotiate other creative alternatives so that our role is a better fit for accomplishing ultimate contributions.

Two Major Philosophical Leadership Models

There are two key philosophical leadership models in the New Testament that guide us and challenge us as we consider what our ultimate contributions might be. When we take these two leadership models into consideration, we are on solid ground as we pursue what God is doing with us. The two models are called: the Stewardship Model and the Servant Leader Model.

1. **The Stewardship Model** comes from Jesus' teaching on the issues of personal responsibility and stewardship. Jesus taught a number of parables dealing with this topic (see Matthew 25:14-30 and Luke 19:11-27). The core of this model is recognizing that each one of us will someday give an account for how we used or stewarded what God has given us. As we listen to Jesus' words, we recognize that God has given each leader resources that they are to invest and use in God's kingdom. God will hold each of us accountable for how we used the resources he gave us to bring the kingdom to our present circle of influence. This ultimate accounting takes place when we face God as we step into eternity.

The teaching of Jesus is quite clear. Leaders are expected to build upon abilities, skills, and gifts so as to maximize potential for God's glory. Leaders who fail to invest, grow, and develop the resources will fall into the category of the unfaithful servant who had the "talent" he buried taken away. Leaders will receive rewards for faithfulness in their ministry in terms of abilities, skills, gifts, and opportunities. Jesus pointed out that each of us are uniquely gifted as to gifts and the degree to which the gift can be used effectively, and we have a responsibility to steward them for his glory.

In addition to faithfulness, the effort that we exert to use, develop, and grow the resources God gives us will be measured as well. We see this in the parable Jesus taught in Luke 19. Jesus tells us that we will receive rewards for productivity. What we produce and the results of our efforts count. Our zealousness, passion, and effort are important components and will be evaluated.

The implications and responsibilities that flow out of understanding this stewardship model should lead us to want to achieve what God wants. We should want to be faithful to that which he has entrusted to us and to use it fully for God's glory. I am sure that all of us want to stand before Jesus as we step into eternity ready to give a good accounting. None of us want to end up in the category of the unfaithful servant. The challenge of the stewardship model is that it can produce a driven-ness to accomplish or an unhealthy focus on achieving. A second philosophical leadership model is given in the New Testament to help keep us in balance.

2. The Servant Model of leadership flows out of Jesus' teaching about leadership, primarily in Matthew 20:20-28 and Mark 1:35-45. There are also a number of secondary passages that compliment these primary passages. These include the Parable of the Waiting Servant, Matthew 24:42-51; Luke 12:35-40, 41-48; the Parable of the Unprofitable Servant, Luke 17:7-10; and the Suffering Servant in Isaiah 52:13-53:12.

The core of this leadership model is: In God's kingdom, leaders use their leadership influence to serve the followers. Jesus was the primary example of this kind of leadership. He recognized his relationship to his Father and out of the love relationship with his Father, Jesus submitted himself and his leadership to serving him. In the same way, the Father, out of his love for the Son served his Son by giving him everything he needs to fulfill his ultimate contributions. The Gospel of John points out this intimate mutually serving relationship that existed between the Father and the Son.

What does this example mean for us? First of all, we recognize that all that we do in leadership is an act of service to God. Everything we do is directed toward serving him. Secondly, everything we do in leadership is an act of service to God's people. Leadership is not about us or what we are doing. It is ultimately about God and his people. This kind of leadership model necessitates a kind of sacrifice on the leader's part. To serve God and God's people requires us to sacrifice ourselves to God on behalf of others.

The primary way that we demonstrate this kind of leadership is through modeling. We live out what we hope, expect, and pray for the followers to live out. We lead from the front by living it out in front of them. There is no room for what Jesus called "lording it over the followers." The followers do not exist for us to use in order to accomplish our agenda. Servant leaders exist to lead them by serving them and helping them to accomplish what God wants for their lives. There is little chance of abuse of authority if we function as servant leaders for God.

The anticipated return of Jesus is a major motivation in both of these models. We serve and want to be found serving faithfully because of what Jesus has done for us. We use the resources that he gave us to the best of our abilities. The servant leader model runs counter to worldly leadership models. In the world's systems, leaders expect or even demand special privileges for their leadership. Special recognition, special pay, and special status are just a few of their expectations. Leadership is different in the Kingdom of God. Leaders are motivated by something else. Our love for God and our desire to be like him is what motivates us.

What Should We Do About Ultimate Contributions?

If we understand and operate out of these two philosophical leadership models, we can gain the perspectives about ultimate contributions to our benefit. Here is what I would suggest that you do.

Step 1: *Begin by tentatively identifying your ultimate contribution set.* Use the list that my father has identified to help you (see Appendix E: Ultimate Contributions Inventory). As I mentioned before, we have found that most leaders will have a combination of 2 or 3 different types of ultimate contributions. This forms what we call the ultimate contribution set. Some will be clearer and will be dominant while others may be more secondary. Understanding your giftedness and understanding what God has revealed about your destiny will point you in the direction of making a tentative identification. Remember that your contribution is something that you have already been doing. The ultimate contribution is simply the accumulated daily contributions over your lifetime.

Step 2: *Seek to get some confirmation from God and others who know you about your insights into your contribution set.* Don't just do this on your own. Get people who know you to help you confirm or readjust what you are seeing in your life. A mentor or life coach who is versed in the dynamics of discovering ultimate contributions or leaving a lasting legacy can help with this.

Step 3: *Identify other leaders who have similar contributions.* Look at what God did with them. How did God lead them to make their contributions? This will give you more perspective or ideas of things you can do to move you towards accomplishing what God has designed you to do.

Step 4: *Make a decision to deliberately move towards ministry or ministry roles that will help you focus on the elements of your contribution.* Make decisions that will allow you to focus on them. This process may be gradual or sudden. It is best to be pro-active, but sometimes God initiates sudden changes such as downsizing or illness that forces a leader to explore other options for role fit and effectiveness. Remember, in the end game, spiritual authority is critical for our effectiveness. If you have spiritual authority, you will have many opportunities to influence whether you have a formal leadership position or not.

Living a Life that Counts

I think all of us have reflected on Paul's words to Timothy recorded in 2 Timothy 4:7-8:

> "I have fought the good fight. I have finished the race. I have stayed faithful. And now the prize awaits me, the crown of righteousness, which the Lord, the righteous Judge will give me on the day of His return."

Paul was very aware that the end was near. As we go into the end game, there is a growing awareness that the end is drawing near. We need to become more focused on the finish line. Will we make it? Has it been worth it?

Paul knew what his race was. He knew what he was aiming at. He tells the Corinthians while moving out of the middle game into the end game that he had to discipline himself so that he would not be disqualified (I Corinthians 9:24-27). This kind of focus, resolve, and discipline allows a leader to be intentional about finishing well and leaving a lasting legacy.

Understanding and evaluating your life in regards to your ultimate contribution will help you see and know the course of your race better. You can make course adjustments in order to stay focused.

You are better able to pace yourself and work more efficiently. It will enhance your enjoyment of the race because you know with increased certainty that you are doing what God designed you to do.

You will know that your answer to the master of the house will be, "Look master what I have done with the resources that you gave me to steward for you." And you know that you will receive the rewards that he will give you for your faithfulness and your zealousness for him. That will make it all worth it.

Back to Schmidt

If someone were to make a movie about the end of my life, I imagine a very different ending than the one I watched in this movie. I do not want to spoil it for you, but there was a nice touch at the end that was very moving and heart wrenching. But still, when I walked out of the movie I knew that my ending would be very different.

You see, I have been investing in a cause that is much bigger than me. In fact my ministry is not about me. What I believe will be the end result of my life, the end of the movie of my life, will be a list of contributions and investments that I made in others in the name of Jesus. I want people to remember Jesus in me, working through me. That is what motivates me to make the hard choices and keep moving towards him and his ultimate contributions for my life.

Application and Discussion questions:

1. How have you answered the question, what makes my life worth living?

2. What is your tentative identification of your ultimate contributions?

3. What are the main things that you want to leave behind as a legacy?

4. What steps can you take to further focus your life on accomplishing what God has designed for you?

Chapter 11

Passing the Baton

Jesus, after his resurrection, appeared to his disciples and instructed them:

> "All authority in heaven and earth has been given to me. Therefore go and make disciples of all nations, baptizing them in the name of the Father and of the Son and of the Holy Spirit, and teaching them to obey everything I have commanded you…" Matthew 28: 18-20, NIV

In this passage, he focuses on what I call the Jesus Methodology of Ministry that he demonstrated in his life and ministry so that his disciples would have a model to follow in the completion of his ultimate goal that "this gospel of the kingdom will be preached in

Starting Well

the whole world as a testimony to all nations, and then the end will come" (Matthew 24: 14, NIV).

Jesus' message was the gospel of the kingdom and his methodology was to care for the multitudes while investing in a few faithful followers. Let me try and illustrate this in the following diagram:

Diagram 5: Jesus' Methodology of Ministry

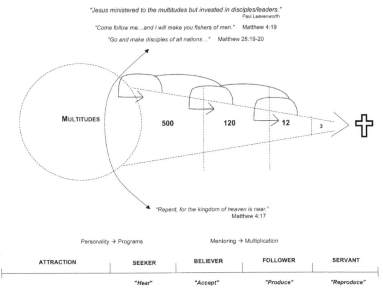

General programs can attract the multitudes where we serve by ministering to their needs. These programs can also serve as a recruitment pool for identifying potential disciples who can be recruited for life transformation and skills training so that they can repeat this relational process with others.

II Timothy 2: 2 challenges leaders to invest in faithful folks who, in turn, will invest in other faithful people. If we desire to become intentional in making disciples and developing leaders, we may want to participate in these types of attraction events where emerging leaders hang out. From these attraction events, we can identify potential leaders and then initiate relational opportunities where growth and development can take place in transforming ways. I will describe this strategy (EI2 Continuum) in greater detail in Chapter 12: Afterglow.

Jesus' Methodology

Jesus embraced both an attraction and discipleship model in his ministry. Let me explain. Jesus seems to be a "both-and" rather than "either-or" thinker and practitioner. He preached, taught, and healed to attract crowds of needy people. Jesus had compassion on them. He was deeply concerned about their needs, but there was more to Jesus' ministry than that. He ministered to the multitudes AND invested in a few:

> "Jesus went through all the towns and villages, teaching in their synagogues, preaching the good news of the kingdom and healing every disease and sickness. When he saw the crowds, he had compassion on them, because they were harassed and helpless, like sheep with out a shepherd. Then he said to his disciples, 'The harvest is plentiful but the workers are few. Ask the Lord of the harvest, therefore, to send out workers into his harvest field." (Matthew 9: 35-38, NIV)

Do you see what is going on here? Jesus attracted large crowds of needy people through his message of good news demonstrated in power through his healing. Jesus did not stop there. He recognized that as one person there is no way that he could meet all the needs represented by this crowd. So, he turned to his disciples and explained his dilemma: the need for more workers.

The harvest was not the problem – it was plentiful! The problem was too few workers. So Jesus told them to pray to the Lord of the harvest to send out workers into his harvest field. That's it, right? We need to pray harder (and louder). NO, prayer was just the beginning. Notice what comes next in this passage:

> "He called his twelve disciples to him and gave them authority to drive out evil spirits and to heal every disease and sickness… These twelve Jesus sent out with the following instructions: '… As you go, preach this message: "The kingdom of heaven is near." 'Heal the sick, raise the dead, cleanse those who have leprosy, drive out demons. Freely you have received, freely give…'" (Matthew 10: 1, 5, 7-8, NIV)

There were no chapter breaks in the original manuscripts of the Bible, so the story that began in Matthew 9 continues into chapter 10. The disciples became the answer to their own prayers for workers. This is the way prayer is suppose to work. As we pray for God's will, we become sensitive to what he wants to accomplish and can participate in some way in its fulfillment.

The disciples were getting on-the-job training so that they would be able to do what Jesus did and train others to do the same, thus expanding the labor force dramatically. It was this multiplication strategy that becomes the launching pad for the completion of the great commission. A closer look at Jesus' methodology of multiplication in the Bible reveals that:

1. Jesus proclaimed "repent, for the Kingdom… is near" (Matthew 4: 17)

2. Jesus prayed about whom to call to be his disciples (Luke 6: 12-16)

3. He invited 12 to be "with" him in life and ministry (Matthew 4: 18-20)

4. He taught them about the reality of "thy Kingdom come" (Matthew 5-7)

5. He modeled for his disciples the character and behavior that he taught them (Matthew 8-9)

6. Jesus ministered in Kingdom power (compassion and miracles) as he responded to God's leading (Matthew 4: 23 and 8-9)

7. He shared his burden for the people with them and commanded them to pray for God to raise up laborers for the harvest (Matthew 9: 35-38)

8. He sent them out 2-by-2 (short-term outreach) in groups of 12 (Matthew 10) and 72 (Luke 10) to practice what he was "training" them for

9. Jesus debriefed the disciples after their short-term outreaches to make sure that they understood the centrality of salvation (not just "power" ministry) to his message and methods (Luke 10)

10. He co-ministered with his disciples in a controlled environment to help them learn by "doing" (Matthew 11-25)

11. He prepared them for his departure and their continued ministry in an uncontrolled environment (John 11-17)

12. He commissioned them (after his crucifixion and resurrection) by his "authority" to do what he did to them ("make disciples") in all nations (Matthew 28: 18-20):
    * Ministry (John 20), Empowered witness (Acts 1), Preaching (Mark 16, Luke 24)

13. Jesus promised to be with them always (Matthew 28: 20)

14. He empowered them with the Holy Spirit (Acts 2) to live and minister as he did in Jerusalem (local), Judea and Samaria (regional), and the ends of the earth (global)

15. Jesus prays for (intercedes) his disciples while in heaven (after his ascension) at the right hand of the Father (Hebrews 7)

16. He is coming again to establish a new heaven and earth (Revelation 21) once his disciples have "evangelized" the entire world (Matthew 24: 14)

This methodology of multiplication resulted in the necessary infrastructure to serve the rapid expansion of the early church described in The Acts of the Apostles. The multiplication strategy of Jesus was not just for his life and ministry. It is a kingdom strategy for the church, even today, until the great commission is completed.

Notice in Acts that Barnabas invested in Paul (Acts 9: 26-30; 11: 22-26; 13: 1-3; 13: 4-14: 28; 15: 1-5; 15: 36-41) who invested in Silas, Timothy, and Titus (Acts 15: 40; Acts 16: 1-6 and I and II Timothy and Titus). In fact, Paul reinforced this strategy when he told Timothy, who was the point leader of a large church:

> "And the things you have heard me say in the presence of many witnesses entrust to reliable men [and women] who will also be qualified to teach others." (II Timothy 2: 2, NIV)

The brilliance of this strategy is revealed in the following comparison between the evangelistic addition (one convert per day) and the discipleship multiplication methodology over a 15-year period (Greg Ogden, *Transforming Discipleship*, p, 137):

Year	Evangelist	Discipler
1	365	2
2	730	4
3	1095	8

4	1460	16
5	1825	32
6	2190	64
7	2555	128
8	2920	256
9	3285	512
10	3650	1024
11	4015	2048
12	4380	4096
13	4745	8192
14	5110	16,384
15	5475	32,768

I use this illustration to show the significance of multiplication over time, not to diminish the importance of evangelism. They are both important and they were intended to go hand in hand. Neither activity stands alone. They compliment each other in a synergetic way.

That is why it is so important to look closely at and learn from Jesus' methodology of ministry. He ministered to the multitudes while focusing on a few who would duplicate this with others. Hopefully, you are becoming convinced of this powerful methodology that Jesus demonstrated and that we can apply in our own lives and ministries.

Not many of us can command the attention of the multitudes through our charisma, dynamic communication skills, or miraculous gifting. There is certainly a place for these gifted few, but most of us do not have these qualities. The Mentoring>Empowering>Multiplication (M>E>M) process is for everyone.

Spiritual mentoring can be described as "intentional relationships" or "friendships with a purpose." Over time, our engagement, invitation, investment, and empowering (EI2) can have a profound impact. Remember Jesus' words, "as you go about your daily affairs, intentionally mentor others who will mentor others, so that eventually we will impact the whole world with the good news of the kingdom" (my paraphrase of Matthew 24: 14 and Matthew 28: 18-20).

Empowering Through Spiritual Authority

Richard described the importance of spiritual authority in the end game in Chapter 9: Spiritual Authority so I will only do a brief review here to give context for understanding its importance in passing the baton to the next generation.

J. Robert Clinton, in *Clinton's Biblical Leadership Commentary*, states that *"effective leaders value spiritual authority as a primary power base"* (p. 440). This is critical to our understanding of passing the baton to other leaders (and especially to younger emerging leaders). Although, there are several influence bases that leaders can use to influence others, spiritual authority is critical because we reproduce in kind. Before commenting further on this let's take a look at other types of influence:

- Force – use of physical and/or psychological force to gain compliance

- Manipulation – use of partial information to gain compliance

- Power – use of personality, competency, position, rewards and/or punishment to gain compliance

- Persuasion – use of verbal skills to gain compliance

By contrast, spiritual authority is the right to influence conferred upon a leader by followers because of their perception of mature spirituality in that leader. Someday you may be in a situation where you do not have a formal position as your base of influence. If you function out of spiritual authority you will always have influence whether you have a formal position or not!

As we saw in Chapter 6: Deep Processing, spiritual authority comes out of humility and brokenness and is characterized by the following:

1. Ultimate source is through Lordship relationship with Christ.
2. Power base is an experiential relationship with God.
3. Primary power form is persuasion or use of word gifts.
4. Ultimate goal of spiritual authority is the growth of people in coming to know Christ and learning to be his disciples.
5. Evaluation of spiritual authority is the quality of character in the leader and the long-term results of growth and spiritual maturity in his/her followers.
6. Submission to God in spiritual authority is non-defensive. The leader does not use force, manipulation, or natural power to influence people.

This is the type of maturity that is demonstrated through the leadership of those who are finishing well. They have learned how to live and lead out of spiritual authority and they want to help younger leaders discover for themselves this same power base.

Leadership Transitions

Passing the baton on to our successor is not an easy task, but it is incredibly important for the continuity and future of the organizations that we have invested in through our leadership.

Unfortunately, few leaders develop succession plans and fewer still actually implement them. There are all sorts of reasons for this:

- Fear of loss of power and control.

- Fear of loss of prestige and prosperity.

- Personal insecurity.

- Uncertainty about retirement.

- Lack of planning.

- Lack of foresight.

Failure to make and implement healthy and effective leadership transitions can cause all sorts of personal and organization difficulties. All you have to do is look at the fall out of the many poor transitions in the Bible or the corporate world. For our purposes here, let's look at some of the poor transitions described in the Bible:

- Judges (Judges 3-13)

- Eli to his sons (I Samuel 4)

- Samuel to Saul (I Samuel 9-15)

- Saul to David (I Samuel 16-19 and I Samuel 31-II Samuel 2)

- David to Absalom (II Samuel 13-15 and 18-19)

- David to Solomon (I Kings 1-2 and 10-11)

- Solomon to his sons (I Kings 12-14)

Without going intro a lot of detail, these transitions were pretty tragic. These stories read more like soap operas than anything: nepotism, intrigue, betrayal, jealousy, rejection, idolatry, immorality, greed, murder, civil strife and war, etc. Pretty nasty stuff! Now contrast these transitions with those that went well:

- Moses to Joshua (Deuteronomy 31)

- Elijah to Elisha (II Kings 2)

- Jesus to his disciples (John 13-21)

- Barnabas to Paul (Acts 9 and 12-13)

- Paul to Silas, Timothy, and Titus (Acts 15-16 and I/II Timothy, Titus)

Quite a different picture here! The transitions were not always smooth, but because the primary leader intentionally transitioned position to a younger leader with spiritual authority as his base, the transition was much smoother and impacting.

From my study of these transition stories and other sources, I have discovered a general understanding of how to transition in ways that empower others and honor God. This has more to do with whom we are than with techniques, but a few general guidelines may be helpful. Transition is inevitable! Leaders transition all the time for a variety of reasons — another job, poor performance, downsizing, out-sourcing, death, etc. — so it is best to be prepared. Here are a few guidelines:

1. Learn how to be an effective mentor throughout life.

2. Sponsor younger leaders along the way and learn from your experience.

3. Prayerfully develop a transition plan in a timely fashion.

4. Seek the counsel of others who have successfully made transitions.

5. Cultivate a leadership development culture within the organization you lead.

6. Prayerfully watch for potential successors within your organization or network.

7. Remember that the true qualities of a leader are best demonstrated in crisis, so watch how your potential successor handles stress.

8. Once you have a successor in mind that is acceptable to other organizational leadership (i.e. boards), begin to share responsibilities.

9. Groom successor through exposure, networking, affirmation, critique, etc. so he/she has a better understanding of the organizational culture and job responsibilities.

10. Once the transition is completed, take a vacation and do not micromanage from the sideline.

11. Pray! Pray! Pray!

12. Be available in healthy ways as a mentor for your successor on an as need basis.

How we transition in leadership will have a significant impact on our legacy and the continued impact of the people and organizations that we once led.

Legacy

I described ultimate contributions briefly in Chapter 8 and Richard described them in greater detail in Chapter 10, so I will keep my comments on legacy brief. As I look back on my life, I have identified three general stages and transitions. My personal transitions have looked something like this:

- Stage 1: Belonging – childhood through early adulthood

- Stage 2: Competency – early adulthood through middle age

- Stage 3: Significance – later middle age through the end of life

It is stage 3: Significance, where issues of legacy become the focus. Has my life and leadership really mattered? What will I be remembered for by my spouse, children, family members, colleagues, community, etc.? How can I impart what I have learned in life and leadership to others? Will they even care?

I could go on and on with questions like this that I have wrestled with over the past few years. The bottom line is - If we have ordered our lives and leadership in such a way so we are finishing well, we have a lot to give! As we transition from positions of responsibility, we will have more time (and less pressure) to insure that we establish a lasting legacy of empowering others.

For me, this has come serendipitously out of some circumstances that I had not planned on which forced me into a position where I have more flex time to focus on writing, teaching, and mentoring. This transition has not been easy as there have been some major financial challenges that God has had to creatively solve for us - so far so good! And we sense that he is with us and will continue to use us for his glory.

Application and Discussion questions:

1. What do you think about Jesus' Methodology of Ministry?

2. What insights have you gained from learning about Jesus' methodology for discipleship and leadership development?

3. What has been your experience in mentoring younger leaders? What have you learned from this?

4. Why do you think spiritual authority is important for effective leadership and healthy transitions?

5. What is your plan for transitioning leadership in your organization?

6. How do you plan to implement this transition plan?

7. What do you hope your legacy will be? What are you actively doing to help make this a reality?

Chapter 12

Afterglow

At the end of the Apostle John's life, while reflecting on his life and legacy, he said:

> "It gave me great joy to have some brothers come and tell about your faithfulness to the truth and how you continue to walk in the truth. I have no greater joy than to hear that my children are walking in the truth." (III John 3-4, NIV)

John, who had seen and accomplished so much in his life, recognized the importance of empowering others as his lasting legacy. His children in the faith would continue the cause that he had given his life for. This is what happens for those who finish well and spend their afterglow years transitioning well and investing in the next generation.

Afterglow is the final stage in Clinton's leadership emergence theory (LET). For those who have remained faithful over the long haul and realized their destiny to a substantial degree (convergence), there is a stage in life and leadership characterized by enjoyment and influence. This stage is rarely attained (in part because so few finish well), but when convergence has been realized and God grants additional years to a Christian leader they can continue to have a major influence through their relationships with others. The primary tasks in this stage are to finish well and pass the baton of leadership on to the next generation.

Spiritual mentoring can be a major influence role and have a profound impact on younger leaders. The establishing of a lasting legacy through the mentoring of others through their life challenges is very important in afterglow. This is a stage in which a Christian leader is able to enjoy the blessings of a life of obedience. From the status of finishing well comes spiritual authority for encouragement and influence of the next generations of disciples and leaders.

Mentoring

Jesus ministered to the multitudes while he invested in a few. Let's take a closer look at how he invested in his disciples in such a way that they were empowered to do what he did so that they can invest in others who will in turn do the same. I call this process spiritual mentoring. Definitions of spiritual mentoring include:

- "Mentoring is a relational experience in which *one person empowers another* by sharing God-given resources" (Clinton, *Connecting*, p. 38).

- Transformational relationships.

- Friendships with Godly purpose and outcome.

I like to think of spiritual mentoring as a relationally based process of empowerment that results in both parties growing spiritually. Spiritual mentoring is mutual and based in a Biblical understanding of relationships that are "mutually submitted to Christ and one another" (Ephesians 5: 21).

Empowerment

What do I mean by empowerment? Empowerment involves transformational relationships in which all participants come to a healthier understanding and experience of their God-given potential as individuals, members of social networks, and members of a community who serve and empower others. Let's look at each aspect of empowerment a little closer:

1. *Transformational Relationships* involve caring and sharing of life experiences and resources.

2. *Mutually Empowering* involves the healthy growth of all parties involved.

3. *Understanding and Experiencing God-Given Potential* involves the transformational work of the Word of God and the Spirit to change us so that we can become more like Christ in character, perspective, and behavior while discovering our uniqueness as God's human creation.

4. *Serve and Empower Others* involves the understanding that realizing our unique potential in God connects us to others in empowering ways through service.

According to J. Robert Clinton (*Connecting*, p. 95-96) there are eight major empowerment functions possible in healthy spiritual mentoring relationships:

1. Encouragement
2. Soundboard
3. Evaluation
4. Perspective
5. Advise
6. Networking
7. Guidance
8. Healing

Sounds great, but you may be a little cautious. Maybe you have been burned in some close relationships and are not very eager to try again. That is understandable, but there are some really good reasons to be involved in spiritual mentoring relationships. Let me suggest a few:

- We are social beings and need healthy relationships.

- We live in a socially dysfunctional culture.

- Our individualism is causing burdens too heavy to hold up under.

- We need others to help us mature as whole people.

- We can save ourselves a lot of "drama" and grief if we can establish healthy accountability.

- We have something to offer others.

The bottom line is that we need one another to be fully human. We were created that way and we realize our full humanity only when we are involved in loving God, one another, and our neighbors.

Spiritual Mentoring Continuum

J. Robert Clinton, in his book *Connecting*, has developed a "Spiritual Mentoring Continuum" (p. 41) that I have adapted here to describe various types of spiritual mentoring:

Intensive Mentoring:

* Discipler – establishing basics of following Christ
* Spiritual Guide – establishing spiritual disciplines
* Spiritual Trainer – motivation and ministry skill development
* Internship (Apprenticeship) – on-the-job training

Occasional Mentoring:

* Counselor – Biblical perspective and advice for relationships, circumstances, and ministry
* Adviser – provides wisdom from life experience to help gain perspective for life/ministry decision making
* Coach – helps draw out inner resources for problem solving, vision, and/or life planning
* Teacher – knowledge and understanding of particular subject
* Sponsor – career guidance, protection, and promotion

Passive and Distant Mentoring:

* Divine Contact – person, word, and/or circumstances used to confirm God's will
* E-Mentoring – computer-based mentoring
* Contemporary Model – living model for life and ministry
* Historical Model – non-living model for life and ministry

Intensive spiritual mentoring tends to be short-term in duration, involving regular meetings for empowerment in specific areas of spiritual and leadership growth. Occasional spiritual mentoring tends to be based on a need-to-know basis or opportunity basis involving specialized issues. Passive and Distant spiritual mentoring involves vicarious empowerment. We may not have any relationship with the person, but can still learn from their teachings or life examples.

Most leaders can function in at least one, possible more, of these spiritual mentoring types depending on giftedness, calling, and availability. Connecting with other people in non-formal roles might be unfamiliar at first, but there are many leaders, especially, younger emerging leaders who would love to have a relationship with an experienced leader who is finishing well. Many of us do not know how to go about this. Again, let's take a look at Jesus' example and see what we can learn from him.

Mentoring>Empowering>Multiplication

Matthew 28: 18-20 is often referred to as the "great commission," but it is actually one of several commissions that Jesus gave to his disciples. This particular commission focuses on what I call the Mentoring>Empowering>Multiplication dynamic that Jesus demonstrated in his life and ministry so that his disciples would have a model to follow in the completion of his ultimate goal that "this gospel of the kingdom will be preached in the whole world as

Afterglow

a testimony to all nations, and then the end will come" (Matthew 24: 14, NIV).

God's message is the gospel of the kingdom and his methodology is Mentoring>Empowering>Multiplication (M>E>M). Based on the M>E>M process I have developed an intentional strategy for its implementation. I call it the EI2 Continuum and it looks like this:

Diagram 6: Mentoring>Empowering>Multiplication

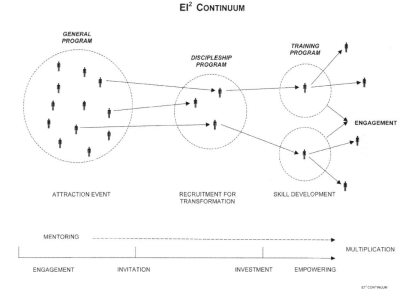

Note here that the backdrop of this diagram is Jesus' methodology of ministry model that we looked at in Chapter 11: Passing the Baton. The basis for this diagram is the observation that Jesus ministered to the multitudes while investing in a few faithful followers (who would duplicate this with others...).

With this in mind, let's take a closer look at Diagram 6. Effective attraction events meet the felt needs of people in caring ways. This is critical. These types of events cannot be used as a recruitment program alone. They need to be genuine events designed to meet people's real needs. These types of events will probably attract some who want to go to the next level in their discipleship. So, in the context of an attraction event, potential disciples may be identified.

What are the characteristics of potential disciples who we may want to help empower? Who are we looking for? The following characteristics of potential leaders can serve as a grid for identifying potential disciples to invest in.

Characteristics of Potential Leaders:

1. Faithful and able to follow through over time
2. Teachable and willing to be accountable
3. Servant orientation and willingness to do the "dirty" work
4. Appetite and application orientation toward the Word of God
5. Orientation toward growing in holiness/righteousness through the practice of the classical disciplines of grace
6. Orientation toward "hearing" and applying the voice of God
7. Self-starting motivation

Perspective disciples (and especially leaders who emerge out of discipleship pools) will not have all of these characteristics, but should have some with faithfulness and being teachable as primary characteristics. Remember from our study of II Timothy 2: 2 that we are to invest in faithful folks who, in turn, will invest in other faithful people. If we desire to become intentional in making disciples and developing leaders, we may want to participate ("engagement") in these types of attraction events. From these attraction events, we can identify potential disciples and leaders and then initiate ("invite") relational opportunities where growth and development ("investment") can take place in transforming ways ("empowering").

CAUTION: Generally, it is best (and safest) for men to mentor men and women to mentor women (see Titus 2). Cross gender mentoring is not forbidden in the Bible, BUT there are certain challenges and vulnerabilities that must be considered honestly and carefully. **Bottom line – as spiritual mentors we need to be "above reproach" in all of our actions and relationships** (see I Timothy 3: 1-7, especially verse 2).

I have been coming at this M>E>M process from several angles to reinforce the intentional process that Jesus modeled and that we can appropriate. Hopefully, you are becoming convinced of this powerful methodology that Jesus demonstrated and that we can apply in our own lives and ministries.

Not many of us can command the attention of the multitudes through our charisma, dynamic communication skills, or miraculous gifting. There is certainly a place for these gifted few, BUT most of us do not have these qualities. The M>E>M process is for everyone. Remember, spiritual mentoring can be described as "intentional relationships" or "friendships with a purpose." Over time, our engagement, invitation, investment, and empowering (EI2) can have a profound impact.

Remember Jesus' words, "as you go about your daily affairs, intentionally mentor others who will mentor others, so that eventually we will impact the whole world with the good news of the kingdom" (my paraphrase of Matthew 24: 14 and Matthew 28: 18-20).

Establishing Healthy Mentoring Relationships

Now that we have described spiritual mentoring, empowerment, and the EI2 continuum we can move on to the practical steps in establishing healthy spiritual mentoring relationships. J. Robert Clinton, in his book *Connecting*, uses "The Ten Commandments of Mentoring" (p. 197-198) as a helpful guide for establishing, maintaining, and transitioning mentoring relationships in healthy ways.

Phase 1 - *Establishing Mentoring Relationships:*
Commandment 1: **Relationship** – establish the mentoring relationship. There are several variables that are important to understand in establishing mentoring relationships. They include attraction, chemistry, being teachable, and faithfulness:

- Attraction – like gift mixes (spiritual gifts, natural abilities, and acquired skills) tend to be attracted to each other.

- Chemistry – some types of personalities work well together and others do not.

- Being Teachable – the potential for transformational growth tends to be linked to one's appetite for and willingness to change.

- Faithfulness – people tend to get out of a relationship what they invest in it.

These variables are important to consider before establishing mentoring relationships. It is wise to be aware and consider these variables before committing to a mentoring relationship.

Commandment 2: **Purpose and Expectations** – jointly agree upon the purpose of the mentoring relationship. Unmet expectations are the primary killer of the potential for growth in a mentoring relationship and can lead to disappointment, dysfunction,

Afterglow

and premature termination. Careful attention to purpose and expectations can set the stage for understanding and maximum impact!

A written contract can be helpful here (but not necessary). This sounds pretty formal, but it can save a lot of confusion and even hurt. If you decide to use a contract, it should include written purpose and expectations, times and length of meeting, homework assignments, etc. If you feel uncomfortable with a written contract you should at least talk through these issues before committing to a mentoring relationship.

Phase 2 - *Maintaining Mentoring Relationships:*
Commandment 3: **Regularity** – determine the regularity and types of interactions. Setting dates, times, and length of meetings are part of this, but you also need to address the types of interaction and appropriateness of interactions outside of the mentoring relationship. Issues like social interactions and when it is O.K. to call are all variables that you will have to address sooner or later.

Commandment 4: **Accountability** – determine the type of accountability. What do you do if a mentor or mentoree no shows for an appointment? What do you do if a mentoree does not do their homework assignment before a scheduled meeting? What if they are not doing their best on the homework assignments? What do you do? Let me suggest a couple of questions that may help here:

1. Did you make your expectations clear?
2. If so, did the mentoree hear them?
3. Have you let things go in the past so that the mentoree does not take the commitments seriously?
4. Are there special circumstances that may have contributed to lack of follow through?
5. What adjustments need to be made so that there is not a repeat?

Commandment 5: **Communication** – set up communication mechanisms. You will not have to confront issues as often if you establish clear expectations and communication mechanisms at the start of the relationship. Setting up specific times for feedback and evaluation are helpful, but regular times of praise and the celebration of success are also critical.

People tend to learn best in environments where they are affirmed in honest and loving ways. As a classroom teacher over the years, I have learned that my students tend to step up when they know I believe in them, encourage them, and take pride in their accomplishments. It is the same with healthy mentoring relationships. Healthy communication is more than words; it also involves an attitude of love and affirmation.

If confrontation is necessary, approach it prayerfully and give the other person the benefit of the doubt. There may be circumstances that you are unaware of that are contributing to the problem. The bottom line, though, is that a person has to learn to take personal responsibility for their lives regardless of circumstances if they want to grow and mature.

Commandment 6: **Confidentiality** – clarify confidentiality. We need to create safe environments for our mentoring relationships and this partially involves issues of confidentiality. Be careful here to not fall into the trap of TOTAL confidentiality. You want to be able to talk to appropriate others if you are in over your head or if there are legal issues involved.

Commandment 7: **Life Cycle** – establish the time frame for the mentoring relationship. This helps define the phases of the mentoring relationship so that folks are prepared for the eventual closure of the spiritual mentoring relationship. Remember that intensive spiritual mentoring relationships tend to involve regular meetings over a specific time frame (i.e. three months or six months) while occasional spiritual mentoring relationships tend to be on a need-to-know basis and may be more sporadic.

During the agreed upon time frame it is important to communicate regularly about how the relationship is going and to revisit the purpose and expectations of the relationship (if needed).

Commandment **8: Evaluation** – periodically evaluate the relationship. Regular evaluation can help monitor progress and clarify expectations. Even if you are clear about expectations at the start of the relationship, things change. Perceptions change, circumstances change, anything (and sometimes everything) can change.

Periodic evaluation may lead to adjustments in the time frame or even the expectations of the relationship, and can lead to a much more effective outcome.

Commandment **9: Modification** – modify expectations to reflect real-life circumstances. You may need to slow down or change the focus of your expectations because of what is happening in and/or outside the mentoring relationship. If something is not working, evaluate and modify. Sometimes some pretty creative and helpful modifications can come out of frustration or even failure when the mentor and mentoree stay connected through healthy communication, evaluation, and modification.

Phase 3 - *Transitioning Mentoring Relationships:*

Commandment **10: Closure** – bring timely closure to formal mentoring relationship. This can be a pretty critical phase in the mentoring relationship and can potentially be hurtful if not handled well. Clear expectations about the duration of the spiritual mentoring relationship are important, but gradual transitioning can also be very helpful.

As the end of the mentoring commitment nears, it is important to clarify closure and relational issues. You can become pretty close in spiritual mentoring relationships and may want the friendship to continue even though the type of relationship will change. You may not develop a friendship that lasts into the future. That is O.K. as well.

These relational issues need to be worked through in ways that are honest, open, and mutually agreeable (as much as possible). The bottom line is that transitions can be difficult and expectations can get fuzzy. Again, setting clear expectations at the start, maintaining good communication, regular evaluation and modification (if needed) can help minimize potential misunderstanding and hurt during times of transition and closure.

Nine Things to Do in Afterglow

J. Robert Clinton describes Nine Afterglow activities in three general categories: people ministry, organizational ministry, and special ministry. These activities are applicable for both ministry and marketplace leaders during afterglow. Let's take a look at each category and the activities associated with each.

Three People Ministry Activities:

1. *Correspondence* – timely letter writing, e-mails, phone calls, Skype, texting, etc. can be very encouraging for family, friends, and younger emerging leaders. It does not take a lot – it is often the thought that counts!

2. *Mentoring* – we have already said quite a lot about this, but I cannot emphasize enough how important this can be for all ages of leaders, especially younger emerging leaders.

3. *Financial Support* – helping a loved one through college or grad school, making it possible for a young couple to get away for a weekend, donating toward a building project, etc. are examples of ways that we can share financially and be a blessing in our afterglow years. There are an infinite number of opportunities and options to share financially with others as we learn to be sensitive to God's leading in this area.

Two Organizational Ministry Activities

4. *Boards* – we can use our expertise and influence to help organizations maximize there potential. Timely advise, accountability, resourcing, networking, and encouragement are just a few of the resources we can provide leaders and their organizations during afterglow.

5. *Form On-Going Institutional Trusts* – we can set up trusts or scholarships to help fund organizations and people who have characteristics that we value, thus, we can establish a legacy that can live on for generations to come.

Four Special Ministry Activities

6. *Public Speaking* – filling in for a vacationing pastor, conducting seminars, and teaching at the local community college are just a few examples of ways that we can continue to use our word gifting to encourage and equip others. There are many smaller venues begging for experienced leaders to help out (usually for very little pay) and who knows what our faithfulness in little things might yield for the kingdom!

7. *Writing and Other Artistic Expressions* – we may have files of notes that we have collected over the years or the great American novel that we always intended to write but never seemed to have the time or energy. We may have latent potential as a musician, actress, or artist. Any of these activities could lead to great fulfillment and new opportunities to connect with people in our communities.

8. *Intercession* – standing in the gap for God's preferred future for loved ones, our communities, country, and the world is a significant activity in afterglow. I am convinced that not

much of kingdom value is accomplished on earth unless it is won in heaven through faithful prayer and intercession.

9. *Focused Intimacy with God* – becoming more loving, generous, and kind to family, friends, and strangers is a lasting legacy that is the goal of those who desire to finish well. During afterglow there is the time and opportunity to go deeper in intimacy with God and to apprentice others as a spiritual guide.

Some Final Comments

Most leaders who experience convergence and transition well into afterglow will serve in more than one of these activities depending on gifting, calling, financial resources, health, and their social base.

Prayerful consideration of opportunities is critical for remaining focused on your unique purpose, role, methodologies, and ultimate contributions for finishing well and leaving a lasting legacy.

There may be a let down once a leader let's go of daily responsibilities associated with positional leadership during convergence. This can lead to a sense of isolation, loneliness, or being unappreciated. Be careful here. Just because you do not have a position does not mean that God does not value you and have significant ministry for you. In fact, he does!

Stay involved in people's lives and service and God will open the right doors for you to impact your loved ones and the next generation of leaders so that you will finish well and leave a lasting legacy of a life well lived and leadership that really mattered.

Application and Discussion questions:

1. What is afterglow and what opportunities to leave a lasting legacy does it afford?

2. What is mentoring? Why is it so important in afterglow?

3. Which of the various mentoring roles have you experienced? Which do you feel that you are most effective in?

4. How are you mentoring others now? What are your plans for mentoring in the future?

5. What insights have you gained concerning establishing healthy mentoring relationships?

6. Which of the nine afterglow activities are you currently involved in? Which do you plan to get involved in the future?

7. What do you want to be remembered for when you are dead and gone?

Appendix A: Characteristics of Biblical Elders (adapted from *Elders and Leaders* by Gene Getz, p. 233-236)

1. **First Official Appointments** – When local churches are established, the first official appointments should be spiritual leaders who are able to give overall direction to the church; however, they should not be appointed until they are qualified.

2. **A Unified Team** – The goal of every local church should be to eventually appoint qualified leaders who serve together as a unified team.

3. **Qualifications** – All spiritual leaders should be appointed based on the maturity profile outlined by Paul in the Pastoral Epistles.

4. **Basic Ethics and Morality** – When looking for qualified leaders to serve the church, consider first those men and their families who've grown up in an environment where their values have been shaped by Judeo-Christian ethics and morality.

5. **An Initial Leader** – If there are no candidates in the church who are qualified to serve as official spiritual leaders, another qualified leader needs to serve in either a

temporary or permanent role until others in the church are sufficiently equipped to serve in this role.

6. **A Primary Leader** – Every group of spiritual leaders needs a primary leader who both leads and serves, and who is accountable to his fellow spiritual leaders.

7. **Titles** – When determining titles for spiritual leaders in the local church, how they function is far more important than what the local body calls them.

8. **Multiple Fathers** – Spiritual leaders should manage and shepherd the church just as fathers are to care for their families and shepherds are to tend their sheep.

9. **Important Priorities** – All spiritual leaders should make sure they manage and shepherd the church well by maintaining six important priorities: teaching the word of God, modeling Christ-like behavior, maintaining doctrinal purity, disciplining unruly believers, overseeing the material needs of the church, and praying for the sick.

10. **Mutual Accountability** – Spiritual leaders in the church should hold each other accountable for their spiritual lives as well as the way they carry out their ministries.

11. **Expanded Accountability** – Every body of local church leaders should have some kind of accountability system that extends beyond them – particularly involving the primary leader.

12. **Qualified Assistants** – In order to maintain their priorities, spiritual leaders should appoint qualified assistants who can help them meet the needs of all believers in the church.

13. **Financial Support** – Spiritual leaders are to make sure that those who devote significant amounts of time to

ministry, particularly in teaching the word of God, should be cared for financially.

14. **Adequate Forms** – Spiritual leaders are responsible to make sure that adequate forms are developed to carry out the functions inherent in the above biblical principles.

Appendix B: Spirit-Empowered Leader (from *The Spirit-Empowered Leader Workbook* by Paul Leavenworth)

> "But you will receive power when the Holy Spirit comes on you; and you will be my witnesses in Jerusalem, and in all Judea and Samaria, and to the ends of the earth." (Acts 1: 8, NIV)

This passage is the primary focus and the structure for the book of Acts. When the Holy Spirit comes in Acts 2, it begins a chain reaction in Jerusalem and expands through Judea and Samaria, and ultimately to the ends of the earth. It is the practical outcome of Jesus' words to his disciples before his death on the cross:

> "And this gospel of the kingdom will be preached in the whole world as a testimony to all nations, and then the end will come." (Matthew 24: 14, NIV)

This is the context in which we need to understand what it means to be a spirit-empowered leader. We are part of something bigger than what we perceive and experience in our "here and now." We are to be empowered "witnesses" (Acts 1: 8) to the reality of "God's kingdom come, on earth as it is in heaven" (Matthew 6: 10, paraphrase). This is to be our testimony to the nations!

What does it mean to be a witness like this? The word used for witness (*martus*) in Acts 1: 8 literally means, "martyr, one who bears 'witness' by his [her] death..." (Vine, *Vine's Complete Expository Dictionary of Old and New Testament Words*, p. 680). It also has a forensic or legal sense and means to tell the truth about your experience related to the subject about which you are testifying. The Apostle Paul describes this in terms of our lives being like "jars of clay." He says:

> "But we have this treasure ("Spirit," see II Corinthian 3: 17-18) in jars of clay that this all-surpassing power is from God and not from us. We are hard pressed on every side; but not crushed; perplexed; but not in despair; persecuted; but not abandoned; struck down; but not destroyed. We always carry around in our body the death of Jesus ('cross," see Luke 14: 27), so that the life of Jesus ("resurrection," see I Corinthians 15: 20-22) may also be revealed in our body. For we who are alive are always being given over to death for Jesus' sake, so that his life may be revealed in our mortal body."(II Corinthians 4: 7-11, NIV)

Do you see what is going on here? The resurrection power of God is manifest through our death to self. As we learn to be grace "martyrs", we experience the power of God to transform and release his spirit in authority through us. We essentially become the living dead. His "all-surpassing power" CONTROLS (Ephesians 5: 18) us in such a way that we are (and are becoming) "new creations [in Christ]" (II Corinthians 5: 17). Old, sinful patterns (see Galatians 5: 19-21 can be broken (see Romans 6: 4). We can learn to live the abundance (John 10: 10), manifest by the "fruit of the spirit" (Galatians 5: 22-23) and the "greater works" (see John 14: 12) that Jesus promised to his disciples.

With this in mind, let's take a look at the characteristics of the spirit-empowered life. Let me comment briefly on seven of them:

1. Receiving the Holy Spirit ("seal") at conversion.

2. Filling ("control") of the Holy Spirit for life transformation ("sanctification").

3. Empowering for impacting/equipping others through gift mix (spiritual gifts, natural abilities, and acquired skills).

4. Revelation ("voice of God") for personal and leadership focus and intentionality.

5. Vision for leadership effectiveness ("fruit" and "much fruit").

6. Resources ("abiding") to finish well in life and leadership.

7. Eternal impact through fulfillment of ultimate contributions.

These summaries are reviews from material from *The Spirit-Empowered Leader Workbook*, so this section serves as an overview of the key concepts that I have already covered in another resource (see *Resource* section of this book for additional material on Leadership Development and Finishing Well).

First, **we receive the Holy Spirit ("seal") at conversion.** The primary Bible passage that we looked at was Ephesians 1: 13. Seal (*sphragis*), in this passage, is a verb connected to the word believed (*pisteuo*) and literally means "believing, you were sealed with the Holy Spirit." With the act of believing comes this "seal" deal. They are connected. So, what does seal mean?

Vine (*Complete Expository Dictionary of Old and New Testament Words*) says that:

> "*Sphragis* denotes (a) a seal or signet [ring]... an emblem of ownership and security, here combined with that of destination... the person to be 'sealed' being secured from destruction and marked for reward... the same three indications are conveyed in Ephesians 1: 13... at the time of their regeneration, not after a lapse of time in their spiritual life..." (p. 553)

The seal was used in a variety of activities in the Bible. In the Old Testament, seals were used to identify parties in a pledge (Genesis 38: 18); as decorations for priestly garb (Exodus 28: 11); and as sealing of letters (I Kings 21: 8). In the New Testament, seals were used to seal up scrolls and to ratify a covenant promise or business deal. For our purposes today, seals can be compared to a handshake of promise between parties who trust one another or a signature on a binding contract.

With the "seal" of the Holy Spirit, we have available to us all the resources that we need to become spirit-empowered leaders. We lack nothing in terms of resources. Where we struggle is in application. We have to learn how to activate the resources available through the Holy Spirit for transformation and effectiveness in life and leadership.

Second, **we need to learn how to be filling ("control") with the Holy Spirit for life transformation ("sanctification")**. Sanctification (*qadesh* in the Hebrew and *hagiazo* in the Greek) means, "to be separate, set apart" (Young, *Analytical Concordance to the Bible*, p. 834). Vine (*Vine's Complete Expository Dictionary of Old and New Testament Words*) describes "sanctification" (Greek noun form, *hagiasmos*) as:

> "(a) separation to God, I Corinthians 1: 30; II Thessalonians 2: 13; I Peter 1: 2; (b) the course of life befitting those so separated, I Thessalonians 4: 3, 4, 7; Romans 6: 19, 22; I Timothy 2: 15; Hebrews 12: 14. Sanctification is that relationship with God into which men [women] enter by faith in Christ, Acts 26: 18; I Corinthians 6: 11, and to which their sole title is the death of Christ, Ephesians 5: 25, 26; Colossians 1: 22; Hebrews 10: 10, 29; 13: 12 (p. 545)."

For our review here, let me say that:

1. Sanctification involves a "separation" to God from sin, the fallen world system, and the influences of the devil;

2. Sanctification involves the work of the Holy Spirit in transforming the believer from the inside out; and

3. Sanctification involves obedience to the Word and the leading of the Spirit in the individual life choices of the believer.

Again, we are faced with the problem of the heart, but that is not the only challenge for the believer in his/her journey into sanctification. Although, we are the main problem in this, we also have to contend with a fallen world system and the influences of the devil. The Bible states that:

> "Our struggle is not against flesh and blood, but against rulers, against the authorities, against the powers of this dark world and against the spiritual forces of evil in the heavenly realms." (Ephesians 6: 12, NIV)

I do not want to say much more about this here, but the believer must "work out his [her] salvation" (Philippians 2: 12) in the midst of these three arenas: the flesh, the world, and the demonic.

The good news is that God has given us the power resources we need to gain victory in all of these arenas of life and ministry. The Bible states that we are "more than conquerors through him who loved us" (Romans 8: 37, NIV). Sanctification is a process that begins at salvation, increases throughout life, is completed at death/the return of Christ, and is never fully completed in this life (Grudem, *Bible Doctrine*, chapter 23: Sanctification), but significant progress is possible! We are no longer slaves to sin! We are "new creations" in Christ (II Corinthians 5: 17). We no longer have to be defined by our self-centeredness!

Third, **we need to discover how to be empowering for impacting/equipping others through our gift mix**. Our gift mix is comprised of:

- Spiritual Gifts

- Natural abilities

- Acquired Skills

Spiritual Gifts - Clinton (*The Making of a Leader*, p. 255) defines a spiritual gift as "a God-given unique capacity imparted to each believer for the purpose of releasing a Holy Spirit empowered ministry via that believer." The Bible describes spiritual gifts (*charisma*) in Romans 12: 3-8; I Corinthians 12-14; Ephesians 4: 11-13; and I Peter 4: 8-11. It is important to note that in all of these passages, the authors state or infer that spiritual gifts must be exercised in love in order to be effective and impacting.

What are the spiritual gifts mentioned in the Bible? Clinton (*Clinton's Biblical Leadership Commentary*, p. 620-621) divides the gifts into three general categories: word gifts, love (compassion) gifts, and power gifts. I will use the phrase "compassion gifts" for his love gifts as all gifts are intended to be love gifts. Let's take a look at the spiritual gifts represented in each of these categories:

- Word gifts – exhortation, teaching, apostleship, ruling (leadership), prophecy, faith, pastor, evangelism, word of wisdom, word of knowledge

- Compassion gifts – governments (administration), giving, mercy, helps (service), pastoring, evangelism, healing, word of wisdom, word of knowledge

- Power gifts – faith, word of knowledge, discerning of spirits, miracles, tongues, interpretation of tongues, healing, word of wisdom, prophecy

Clinton's lists are from the King James Version of the Bible so I have given the NIV translation for a couple of them in parentheses. Each category has a primary purpose:

Appendix B

- Word gifts > Understanding

- Compassion gifts > Care

- Power gifts > Demonstration

Also, note that there is an overlap in the lists because some of the gifts have more than one function. For example, the gift of pastoring is included in the word and compassion gifts list because this gift functions to bring understanding and care for those being impacted.

Natural Abilities - Let's now move on to the second aspect of gift mix: natural abilities. I will not go into this very much except to say that we all have abilities that we discover and develop over time. Natural abilities might include athleticism, artistic skills, language abilities, math and science orientations, being a people person, and multiple others. Have you ever heard someone say, "You're a natural at _____" (fill in the blank). That is an example of a natural ability. We all have them. Some are more aware of them than others, but we all have them (and they are part of who we are and our destiny). There is overlap between natural abilities and acquired skills. It is hard to know which is which, so I will cover competencies that are important for effective and impacting leadership in the next section on acquired skills.

Acquired Skills - This leads us to our final aspect of gift mix: acquired skills. The distinction between natural abilities is subtle. Natural abilities are already part of us and need to be discovered and developed, while acquires skills are something that we have to learn along the way. Either way, we need them and can develop them over time.

Fourth, **we need revelation ("voice of God") for personal and leadership focus and intentionality**. Revelation is both general (creation, morality) and special (Christ, the Bible, Holy Spirit). Special revelation is the source out of which we learn how to hear God's voice. His "sheep hear his voice" (John 10: 4).

Starting Well

Learning to know God and hear his voice involves communication and communication involves the accurate sending and receiving of information between people. Most of us have little difficulty with the sending part of communication. It is easy for us to make our needs know to others and/or to God. Where most of us have difficulty is in the receiving part of communication. We have a hard time listening to others and/or God. God has given us his word, his son, and his spirit as sources to know him and know his will. But most of us have a difficult time knowing how to use these resources in our daily lives.

Dick Eastman, in his *Challenge the World School of Prayer Manual* (p.159-167), gives 14 principles of divine guidance that may be helpful in clarifying some of the confusion surrounding hearing the voice of God. These include:

1. It is possible to hear God's voice - Colossians 1:9
2. The purpose of all guidance is to know the Lord Jesus intimately - Philippians 3:20
3. God speaks from where He dwells - Luke 17:21
4. The Holy Spirit is heaven's representative in all true guidance - John 16:13
5. God's word is the final judge in all guidance - II Peter 1:19-20
6. Guidance from God is always accompanied by the peace of God - Philippians 4:6-7
7. God speaks through various means (Biblical examples include prayer, visitations, voices, visions, dreams, prophecy, circumstances, etc.)
8. Most guidance from God comes unawares - Psalms 25:9
9. There are several sources of guidance (see #7 above)
10. Hearing God speak must prompt us to action - James 2:17

11. Divine guidance comes from meeting God's demands - Isaiah 58:10-11
12. Divine guidance does not mean that we will know the future - James 5:7-8
13. Guidance is not always pleasant - James 1:2-4
14. Guidance is a skill to be learned - Luke 11:1

WARNING: The "voice of God" will never contradict the "word of God" revealed in the Bible!

As we learn to discern God's voice, we will gain a clearer sense of his presence in and purpose for our life and leadership.

Fifth, **we need Godly vision for leadership effectiveness** ("fruit" and "much fruit"). Learning to hear God's voice and vision are part of the same process and are critical for our effectiveness as spirit-empowered leaders.

Barna (editor, *Leaders on Leadership*) defines vision as a "mental portrait" of God's "preferable future" or "a view of the kind of world God wants us to live in" (p. 47-48). In another book (*The Power of Vision*), he describes four prerequisites (chapter 6: Capturing God's Vision) and nine characteristics (chapter 7: The Character of God's Vision) of Godly vision. First, let's look at the prerequisites:

1. We need to **know God** – primarily through learning obedience to his word and prayer.

2. We need to **know ourselves** – strengths/weaknesses, personality type, leadership style, gift mix, etc.

3. We need to **know our environment** – culture, values, vision, resources of the organization we serve and lead in.

4. We need to **verify the vision** – check with the truths of the Bible and seek wise counsel.

Humility and submission to God is critical in all of these prerequisites. Remember, "we see but a poor reflection" of reality (I Corinthians 13: 12, NIV) even in Godly vision and would be wise to learn to discern the timing (remember what happened to Joseph when he shared the vision prematurely – Genesis 37), team, resources, and strategy. Often, the vision is just the beginning of a faith process that may bring us to the end of our own recourses before God comes through to fulfill his purposes through our vision. Barna gives nine characteristics of Godly vision that are helpful as we try to formulate this important aspect of spirit-empowered leadership:

1. Vision is inspiring for the leader and his/her followers.
2. Vision is change-oriented.
3. Vision is challenging.
4. Vision is empowering.
5. Vision is long-term.
6. Vision is unique to the leader and his/her followers.
7. Vision is strategic and detailed.
8. Vision reveals a promising future.
9. Vision is people-oriented.

Godly vision will take God to fulfill it. We have a role to play. We will have responsibilities to fulfill. And there will be rewards along the way and at the finish line, but we will not be able to complete God's vision without God's resources. Remember Jesus' promise to his disciples:

"I am the vine; you are the braches. If a man [woman] remains in me and I in him [her], he [she] will bear much fruit; apart from me you can do nothing."(John 15: 5, NIV)

Sixth, **we have the resources ("abiding") of the Holy Spirit to finish well in life and leadership.** See Chapter 1: Finishing Well for more information about finishing well.

Last, **we can have eternal impact through fulfillment of ultimate contributions.** See Chapter 10: Ultimate Contributions and Legacy for more information about ultimate contributions.

I trust that this brief overview of what it means to be a spirit-empowered leader who does the "greater works" that Jesus talked about will help spur you on to becoming all that God intends for you to be. There is no greater joy in life than to learn "to give up what we cannot have in order to gain what we cannot loose" (Jim Elliot). This is the promise and potential of learning how to be a spirit-empowered leader!

Appendix C: Doubt and Wisdom (from the Book of Job)

What do you do when you are in pain and do not understand what is happening? If you are like me (Paul), you may try and stuff your questions and soldier on. I do not recommend this! It will evidentially catch up with you (as it has with me) and lead to shallowness, emotional and physical health issues, and dysfunctional relationships. We are wired by God to process our whole being when we are in pain: mind, emotions, and body. And Job demonstrated for us how to go about it. Remember Job's primary complaints:

- God's failure to hear him (13: 3, 24; 19: 7; 23: 3-5; 30: 20)

- God is punishing him (6: 4; 7: 20; 9: 17)

- God allows the wicked to prosper (21: 7)

- God is far away and silent (23: 3; 30: 20)

- God won't vindicate him and fix his problems (19: 7; 24: 1)

And not only did he ask questions of God about these complaints, he got pretty emotional, demanding, and shrill! As I have read through Job 3-37 over the years I have been surprised that God did not blast Job with a lightening bolt from heaven. Job really got into it with God and God seems O.K. with that. What is going on here?

Starting Well

James, in his New Testament letter to Jewish Christians who have been scattered among the nations by persecution, stated:

> "If any of you lacks wisdom, he should ask God, who gives generously to all without finding fault, and it will be given to him. But when he asks, he must believe and not doubt, because he who doubts is like a wave of the sea, blown and tossed by the wind. That man should not think he will receive anything from the Lord; he is a double-minded man, unstable in all he does."(James 1: 5-8, NIV)

What is going on here? Is it O.K. to doubt or isn't it? Job seemed to be raising some pretty serious doubts ("complaints") in his rather one-sided conversation with God. What's with this? A couple of things in this passage from James may help answer this question about whether doubt is O.K. or not.

The answer seems to be "yes" and "no". There seem to be at least two types of general doubt being discussed by James:

1. Doubt>Wisdom

2. Doubt>Lack of Belief

One type of doubt leads to wisdom – insight into application of truth for a specific situation. The other leads to lack of belief. What is the difference? The phrase "double-minded" in verse 8 literally means "double-souled" (*dipsuchos,* from *dis* – "twice" and *psuche* - "a soul"). Vine (*Vine's Complete Expository Dictionary*, p. 588) defines *psuche* as:

> "denotes 'the breath, the breath of life,' then 'the soul,' in its various meanings. (a) natural life and body...(b) the immaterial, invisible part of man... (d) **the seat of personality**... (e) the seat of the sentient element in man... (f) **the seat of will and purpose...**" (**bold** added for emphasis)

There is much more going on in this passage than the mental gymnastics of trying to make sense of something. The type of doubt that James is forbidding is the type that questions the character and integrity of God in such a way that a person hardens his or her heart toward God. Unless we can trust God enough to at least give him the benefit of the doubt, we become "double-souled" and unstable.

It appears from our study of Job that God can handle (and he may even welcome) hard questions as long as they do not come from hard hearts (although he can deal with that as well). If you need further persuading on this you may want to do a read through the Psalms. They are full of heart felt questioning (and have proven to be a source of comfort throughout history for many in their times of distress).

Appendix D: Strategic Formation (from *The Spirit-Empowered Leader Workbook* by Paul Leavenworth)

We will take a look at strategic formation (Calling) and its importance in terms of focus, intentionality, and effectiveness in life and leadership. Before we describe strategic formation, let's review our operational definition of leadership as described by J. Robert Clinton (*The Making of a Leader*):

> "Leadership is a dynamic process in which a man or woman with God-given capacity and God-given responsibility influences a specific group of God's people toward God's purpose for that group."

Strategic formation is critical for our understanding and fulfillment of personal and leadership purposes. Barna (*Leaders on Leadership*) states, "Understand that to be a Christian leader, the vision towards which you lead people must be a vision God gives you" (p. 47). We must learn to lead out of a sense ("mental portrait") of God's purposes for our lives and those we serve and lead. Os Guinness,, in his book *The Call*, says it like this:

> "Deep inside our hearts, we all want to find and fulfill a purpose bigger than ourselves. Only such a larger purpose can inspire us to heights we know we could never reach on our own. For each of us, the real purpose is personal and passionate: to know what we are here to do, and why. Kierkegaard wrote in his Journal: 'The thing is to understand myself, to

see what God really wants me to do; the thing is to find a truth which is true for me, **to find the idea for which I can live and die.**'" (p. 3, **bold** in original text)

Discovering our calling and organizing our lives in such a way as to realize it is critical for our fulfillment and fruitfulness as leaders. Henry Blackaby (*Called and Accountable*) is helpful here. He addresses several questions about calling that can help us get a better grasp on the importance of finding and fulfilling our calling:

1. Why does God call us?
2. What is a call?
3. Who are the called?
4. How am I called?
5. When am I called?
6. How do I live out this call?

Let's take a look at each one of these questions a little more closely and attempt to give Biblical and helpful insights.

First, *why does God call us?* For the answer to this question, Blackaby points us to God's original intent for relationship in creating man and woman in his own image (Genesis 1: 27-31). He states that "the entire Bible bears witness to the truth that God, from eternity, chose to work through His people to accomplish his purposes in the world" (p. 7). God created us to partner with him in purposeful ways. Purpose is part of our humanity and calling is our specific purpose.

Second, *what is a call?* Blackaby answers this question by giving a general context for discovering our specific "personal" sense of calling (Unit 2: What is a Call?). He says that:

1. We are called to a relationship with God.
2. We are called to personal and corporate redemption.
3. We are called to participate in mission.

4. God initiates the call.

5. The call is to obedience.

Our specific "personal" call will come out of and from within this general context. A helpful definition of calling (or what J. Robert Clinton calls "destiny") is:

> "an inner conviction arising from an experience or a series of experiences in which there is a growing sense of awareness that God has His hand on a leader in a special way for special purposes." (J. Robert Clinton, *Clinton's Biblical Leadership Commentary*, p. 371)

This is similar to Barna's description of vision as a "mental portrait" of "God's preferred future.".

Next, *who are the called?* We do not need to spend too much time on this question, because the Bible is very clear that every Christian is called in both a general and specific sense. Blackaby says it like this: "**All are the called!** The differences lie not in whether we are called or not, but in the nature of the assignment given by God" (p. 53).

Fourth, *how am I called?* Clinton (*Clinton's Biblical Leadership Commentary*) is again helpful here. He points out that calling in the Bible seems to follow one of four categories (p. 372-373) of "destiny experiences":

Type I – a destiny experience that is awe-inspiring and through which God is sensed directly as acting or speaking (Example: Moses at the burning bush).

Type II – an indirect destiny experience in which some aspect of destiny is linked to some person other than the leader and is done indirectly for the leader who simply must receive its implications (Example: Hannah's promise to give Samuel to God).

Type III – the build up of a sense of destiny in a life because of the accumulation of providential circumstances that indicate God's purpose for the leader (Example: Abram/Abraham's progressive understanding of his destiny).

Type IV - the build up of a sense of destiny in a life because of the sensed blessing of God repeatedly on a life and recognized by others (Example: Joseph's promotions).

Note here that there is not a "one size fits all" formula for discovering one's calling. We may have one or more of these types of destiny experiences as we discover our calling. We may or may not have a dramatic encounter with God, BUT we will all have to walk out our calling in obedience over the long haul. Remember the "little-big" principle of faithfulness in little being the prerequisite for faithfulness in more!

Next, *when am I called?* Again, let's refer to Clinton on this. He has developed a "destiny processing" pattern (*Clinton's Biblical Leadership* Commentary, p. 372) that is helpful:

Stage 1 - preparation
Stage 2 - unfolding revelation
Stage 3 – increasing confirmation
Stage 4 - fulfillment

Again, remember that these stages are contingent upon our obedience, growth, and maturity. Also, remember how spiritual formation (Character), leadership formation (Competencies), and strategic formation (Calling) are integrated as we move toward fulfillment (Clinton calls this "convergence") and the "much fruit" promised to those who "abide in Christ" (John 15: 5-8) and endure God's pruning.

Last, *How do I live out this call?* For our purposes here, let me encourage you to keep obeying God while progressively growing in your understanding and experience. You cannot miss God's calling for your life if you learn how to faithfully follow him in becoming a more loving person who is maturing in his/her character, competencies, and calling as a leader.

For more information about strategic formation (Calling), see *Resource* section in this book, *The Extraordinary Power of a Focused Life*.

Appendix E: Ultimate Contributions Inventory (Adapted from J. Robert Clinton, *Clinton's Biblical Leadership Commentary*, "Legacy – Leaving One Behind", p. 511-513)

Ultimate contributions are "a lasting legacy of a Christian worker for which he or she is remembered and which furthers the cause of [Christ]..." (Clinton, *Clinton's Biblical Leadership* Commentary, p. 404-405).

1. Rate yourself on the importance of the following to you in terms of the type of legacy you want to leave behind:

1 – Critical   2 – High   3 – Average   4 – So So   5 – Minimal

_____ *Character* - setting standards for life and leadership.
_____ *Ministry {Leadership}* - impacting lives through evangelism and/or disciple-making (mentoring).
_____ *Catalytic* - serving as a change agent who helps make the world better.
_____ *Organizational* - leaving behind an organization, institution, or movement that will impact society in kingdom-advancing ways.
_____ *Ideation* - discovering, developing, describing, communicating, or promoting ideas that help others come to or grow in faith.

2. Identify your top 2-3 types of legacy and rate yourself on the importance of the following to you in terms of the role you see yourself functioning in to fulfill your legacy:

Starting Well

1 – Critical 2 – High 3 – Average 4 – So So 5 - Minimal

Character:
_____ SAINT – a person who has a model life: not a perfect one, but a life others want to emulate.
_____ STYLISTIC PRACTITIONER – a person who has a model ministry or organizational style that sets the pace for others and which others want to emulate.

Ministry [Leadership]:
_____ MENTOR – a person who empowers others through individual or small group influence.
_____ PUBLIC RHETORICIAN – a person who empowers others through effective communication to large groups.

Catalytic:
_____ PIONEER – a person who starts apostolic (missionary/entrepreneurial) organizations or enterprises.
_____ CHANGE PERSON – a person who is able to influence cultures to better organizations and or correct social injustice in society.
_____ ARTIST – a person who is able to impact organizations or cultures through innovation and creative breakthroughs.

Organizational:
_____ FOUNDER – a person who establishes a new organization to meet needs or capture the essence of cultural change.
_____ STABILIZER – a person who can help fledgling organizations develop and move toward stability, efficiency, and effectiveness.

Ideation:
_____ RESEARCHER – a person who develops new ideas or concepts from study and/or research.

Appendix E

_____ WRITER – a person who is able to conceptualize, contextualize, and communicate ideas effectively in a written format.

_____ PROMOTER – a person who is able to promote new ideas through motivation and or networking strategies that expand exposure and buy in.

Once you have completed the inventory, identify the 3-5 ultimate contributions that you ranked as most important. Prayerfully think through how they relate to your core values, purpose, and mission statement.

Appendix G

Accountability Inventory

(adapted from Linda Galindo, *The 85% Solution*, "Your Personal Accountability Quotient", p. 225-231)

Rank yourself on the following questions/statements using the following scale:

| 1 – Consistently | 2 – Regularly | 3 – Occasionally |
| 4 – Seldom | 5 – Never | |

1. I currently have spiritual
mentors in my life: 1 2 3 4 5

2. I meet at least once per
month with a spiritual mentor: 1 2 3 4 5

3. I am accountable for the action plans I commit to:	1	2	3	4	5
4. I don't make excuses or blame when I don't meet my goals:	1	2	3	4	5
5. I am open to constructive criticism from my mentor:	1	2	3	4	5
6. I seek advice from my mentors before making difficult decisions:	1	2	3	4	5
7. I am accountable for results even in difficult circumstances:	1	2	3	4	5
8. I am interested in personal growth:	1	2	3	4	5
9. I am interested in developing my leadership potential:	1	2	3	4	5
10. I am a life-long learner:	1	2	3	4	5

Add up your total points (somewhere between 10 and 50) and use the following scale to evaluate you accountability level.

Scale: 10-20 (Healthy Accountability)
      21-35 (Limited Accountability)
      36-50 (Vulnerable)

Resources

Diagram 7: Leader/Breakthru Network

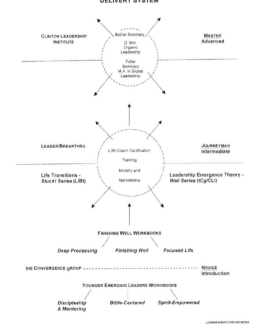

the Convergence group (theconvergencegroup.org)

Leadership Development Series by Paul Leavenworth

The Discipleship and Mentoring Workbook
The Bible-Centered Leader Workbook
The Spirit-Empowered Leader Workbook

Finishing Well Series by Paul Leavenworth,

Finishing Well
Deep Processing
The Extraordinary Power of a Focused Life

Discovery Learning Resources by Paul Leavenworth

Small Group Facilitator Training (DVD)
Focused Life Workshop (DVD)

Coaching

Focused Life Workshop (with 4 follow-up coaching appointments)
Focused Life 1 On 1
L/Bt Coach Certification (with Terry Walling)

The Clinton Institute (jtclintoninstitute.com)

Resources

Leadership Books by J. Robert Clinton
The Making of a Leader
Connecting (with Paul Stanley)

Well Trilogy Series by Richard Clinton and Paul Leavenworth
Starting Well
Living and Leading Well
Finishing Well

Leader/Breakthru (leaderbreakthru.com)

Stuck! Series by Terry Walling
Stuck!
Awakening
Deciding
Finishing

Coaching
TRAC
ReFocusing
L/Bt Coach Certification

Bibliography

Bible Study Resources

The Contemporary Parallel New Testament, 1997, Oxford University Press
The International Standard Bible Encyclopedia, Geoffrey W. Bromiley (editor), 1979, Eerdmans Publishing
Elwell, Walter. Topical Analysis of the Bible, 1991, Baker Books
Vine, W.E. Vine's Complete Expository Dictionary of Old and New Testament Words, 1996, Nelson Publishers

Theology

Boice, James Montgomery. Foundations of the Christian Faith, 1986, InterVarsity Press
Driscoll, Mark and Gerry Breshears. Doctrine, 2010, Crossway
Duffield, Guy. Foundations of Pentecostal Theology, 1987, LIFE
Grudem, Wayne. Bible Doctrine, 1999, Zondervan Publishing
Packer, James. Knowing God, 1973, InterVarsity Press

Theology of the Holy Spirit

Green, Michael. I Believe in the Holy Spirit, 1985, Eerdmans
Lloyd-Jones, Martyn. Joy Unspeakable, 1984, Shaw Publishers
    The Sovereign Spirit, 1985, Shaw Publishers
Wimber, John. Power Evangelism, 1986, Harper & Row
    Power Healing, 1987, Harper & Row
    Power Points, 1991, Harper & Row

Discipleship and Disciple-Making

Arnold, J. Heinrich. Discipleship, 1994, Plough Publishing House
Bailey, Keith. Care of Converts, 1997, Christian Publications
Barna, George. Growing True Disciples, 2000, Issachar Resources
Bonhoeffer, Dietrich. The Cost of Discipleship, 1995, Touchstone/ Simon and Schuster
Briscoe, Stuart. Discipleship for Ordinary People, 1995, Shaw Publishers
Cole, Neil. Cultivating a Life for God, 1999, ChurchSmart Resources
Coleman, Robert. The Master Plan of Discipleship, 1987, Revell Company
Cosgrove, Francis. Essentials of Discipleship, 1988, Roper Press
Drane, John. After McDonaldization, 2008, Baker Books
Eims, Leroy. The Lost Art of Disciple Making, 1978, Zondervan Press
Ferguson, Gordon. Discipling, 1997, Discipleship Publications
Finney, Charles. Principles of Discipleship, 1988, Bethany House Publishers
Grounds, Vernon. Radical Commitment, 1984, Multnomah Press
Hanks, Billie and William Shell (editors). Discipleship, 1981, Zondervan Press
Henrichsen, Walter. Disciples are Made not Born, 1988, Victor Books

Hull, Bill. <u>Building High Commitment in a Low Commitment World</u>, 1995, Revell Company
<u>New Century Disciplemaking</u>, 2001, Revell Company
Kincaid, Ron. <u>A Celebration of Disciple-Making</u>, 1990, SP Publications
Ortiz, Juan Carlos. <u>Disciple</u>, 1995, Charisma House
Petersen, Jim. <u>Lifestyle Discipleship</u>, 2007, NavPress
Rabey, Steve and Lois (editors). <u>Side by Side</u>, 2000, Cook communications
Robertson, Roy. <u>The Timothy Principle</u>, 1986, NavPress
Wallis, Arthur. <u>The Radical Christian</u>, 1981, Revell Company
Watson, David. <u>Called and Committed</u>, 1982, Shaw Publishers

Spiritual Formation

Blackaby, Henry & Claude King. <u>Experiencing God</u>, 1994, Broadman & Holman
Foster, Richard. <u>Celebration of Discipline</u>, 1998, Harper One
Kreider, Larry. <u>Hearing God</u>, 2005, House to House Publications
Lea, Larry. <u>The Hearing Ear</u>, 1988, Creation House
Smith, James Bryan. <u>The Good and Beautiful God</u>, 2009, InterVarsity Press
Stanley, Charles. <u>How to Listen to God</u>, 1985, Nelson Publishers
Tan, Siang-Yang and Douglas Gregg. <u>Disciplines of the Holy Spirit</u>, 1997, Zondervan Publishing
Virkler, Mark. <u>Dialogue with God</u>, 1986, Bridge Publishing
Whitney, Donald. <u>Spiritual Disciplines for the Christian Life</u>, 1991, NavPress
Willard, Dallas. <u>The Spirit of the Disciplines</u>, 1988, Harper & Row
<u>Hearing God</u>, 1999, InterVarsity Press
Willard, Dallas and Don Simpson. <u>Revolution of Character</u>, 2005, NavPress

Brokenness and Humility

John of the Cross (translated and edited by E. Allison Peers). Dark Night of the Soul, 1990, Image Books

Kelly, Thomas. A Testament of Devotion, 1941, Harper & Row Publishers

Murray, Andrew. Humility, 1982, Whitaker House

Nee, Watchman. The Breaking of the Outer Man and the Release of the Spirit, 1997, Living Streams Ministry

Nelson, Alan. Broken in the Right Places, 1994, Thomas Nelson Publishers   Embracing Brokenness, 2002, NavPress

Nori, Don. The Power of Brokenness, 1997, Destiny Image Publishers

Nouwen, Henri. Turn My Mourning Into Dancing, 2001, Word Publishing

Stanley, Charles. The Blessing of Brokenness, 1997, Zondervan

Suffering and Trials

Damazio, Frank. From Barrenness to Fruitfulness, 1998, Regal

Davis, Ron Lee. Gold in the Making, 1983, Thomas Nelson Publishers

MacArthur, John. The Power of Suffering, 1995, Victor Books

Reccord, Bob. Forged by Fire, 2000, Broadman & Holman Publishers

Schaeffer, Edith. Affliction, 1993, Baker Books

Sorge, Bob. Pain, Perplexity and Promotion, 2002, Oasis House

Sproul, R. C. Surprised by Suffering, 1989, Tyndale House

Spurgeon, C. H. The Suffering of Man and the Sovereignty of God, 2001, Fox River Press

Stanley, Charles. How to Handle Adversity, 1989, Thomas Nelson Publishers

Church History

Cairns, Earle. <u>Christianity Through the Centuries</u>, 1982, Zondervan Publishing
Latourette, Kenneth Scott. <u>A History of Christianity</u>, Vol. I & II, 2005, Prince Press
Shelley, Bruce. <u>Church History in Plain Language</u>, 1995, Nelson Publishers

Biographies

Beeson, Ray and Ranalda Mack Hunsicker. <u>The Hidden Price of Greatness</u>, 1991, Tyndale
Edman, V. Raymond. <u>They Found the Secret</u>, 1984, Zondervan
Meyer, F. B. <u>Classic Portraits</u> Series (Abraham, David, Elijah, Israel, Jeremiah, John, Joseph, Joshua, Moses, Paul, Peter, Samuel), reprint 1990, Christian Literature Crusade
Rumph, Jane. <u>Stories From the Front Lines</u>, 1996, Chosen Books
Sciacca, Fran. <u>Wounded Saints</u>, 1992, Baker Books
Skoglund, Elizabeth. <u>Wounded Heroes</u>, 1992, Baker Books
Swindoll, Charles. <u>Great Lives From God's Word</u> Series (David, Esther, Elijah, Jesus, Job, Joseph, Moses, Paul), 1997-2008, Word Publishing
Whittaker, Colin. <u>Seven Guides to Effective Prayer</u>, 1987, Bethany House

Mentoring

Anderson, Keith and Randy Reese. <u>Spiritual Mentoring</u>, 1999, InterVarsity Press
Biehl, Bobb. <u>Mentoring</u>, 1996, Broadman and Holman Publishers

Boshers, Bo and Judson Poling. <u>The Be With Factor</u>, 2006, Zondervan Press
Bruce, A.B. <u>The Training of the Twelve</u>, 1971, Kregel Publications
Clinton, J. Robert and Paul Stanley. <u>Connecting</u>, 1992, NavPress
Coleman, Robert. <u>The Master Plan of Evangelism</u>, 2007, Revell Company
Creps, Earl. <u>Reverse Mentoring</u>, 2008, Jossey-Bass
Davis, Ron Lee. <u>Mentoring</u>, 1991, Nelson Publishers
Elliston, Edgar (editor). <u>Teach Them Obedience in All Things</u>, 1999, William Carey Library
Elmore, Tim. <u>Mentoring</u>, 1998, EQUIP
   <u>The Greatest Mentors in the Bible</u>, 1996, Kingdom Publishing
Engstrom, Ted. <u>The Making of a Mentor</u>, 2005, World Vision
   <u>The Fine Art of Mentoring</u>, 1989, Wolgemuth and Hyatt Publishers
Forman, Rowland, et al. <u>The Leadership Baton</u>, 2004, Zondervan Press
Jones, Laurie Beth. <u>Jesus, Life Coach</u>, 2004, Nelson Publishers
Harkavy, Daniel. <u>Becoming a Coaching Leader</u>, 2007, Nelson Publishers
Hendricks, Howard. <u>As Iron Sharpens Iron</u>, 1995, Moody Press
   <u>Standing Together</u>, 1995, Vision House
Houston, James. <u>The Mentored Life</u>, 2002, NavPress
Krallmann, Gunter. <u>Mentoring for Mission</u>, 1992, GEM
Kreider, Larry. <u>Authentic Spiritual Mentoring</u>, 2008, Regal Books
   <u>The Cry for Spiritual Fathers and Mothers</u>, 2007, House to House Publications
Luce, Ron (editor). <u>Turning the Hearts of the Fathers</u>, 1999, Albury Publishing
Ogden, Greg. <u>Transforming Discipleship</u>, 2003, InterVarsity Press
Otto, Donna. <u>Finding a Mentor, Being a Mentor</u>, 2001, Harvest House
Pue, Carson. <u>Mentoring Leaders</u>, 2005, Baker Books

Schultz, Steve and Chris Gaborit. <u>Mentoring and Fathering</u>, 1996, Christian International Ministries

Stoddard, David. <u>The Heart of Mentoring</u>, 2003, NavPress

Stoltzfus, Tony. <u>Leadership Coaching</u>, 2005, Coach22

Harvard Business Essentials: <u>Coaching and Mentoring</u>, 2004, Harvard Business School Publishing

Christian Leadership

Barna, George. <u>The Power of Vision</u>, 1992, Regal Books

Barna, George (editor). <u>Leaders on Leadership</u>, 1997, Regal Books

Blackaby, Henry and Richard Blackaby. <u>Spiritual Leadership</u>, 2001, Broadman and Holman Publishers

Blackaby, Henry and Kerry Skinner. <u>Called and Accountable</u>, 2002, New Hope Publishers

Clinton, J. Robert. <u>The Making of a Leader</u>, 1988, NavPress
<u>Leadership Emergence Theory</u>, 1989, Barnabas Resources
<u>Clinton's Biblical Leadership Commentary</u>, 1999, Barnabas Publishing

Clinton, Richard and Paul Leavenworth. <u>Starting Well</u>, 1994, Barnabas Publishing

Guinness, Os. <u>The Call</u>, 1998, Word Publishing

Hybels, Bill. <u>Axiom</u>, 2008, Zondervan

Malphurs, Aubrey. <u>Being Leaders</u>, 2003, Baker Books

Maxwell, John. <u>Leadership Gold</u>, 2008, Nelson Publishers

Sande, Ken. <u>The Peacemaker</u>, 2004, Baker Books

Sanders, J. Oswald. <u>Spiritual Leadership</u>, 1994, Moody Press

Stanley, Andy. <u>Visioneering</u>, 1999, Multnomah Publishers

Walling, Terry. <u>Stuck!</u> 2008, ChurchSmart

Marketplace Leadership

Bennis, Warren. On Becoming a Leader, 2003, Basic Books
Blanchard, Ken and Phil Hodges. Lead Like Jesus, 2005, Nelson
Burns, James MacGregor. Leadership, 1978, Harper & Row
Collins, Jim. Good to Great, 2001, Harper Business
Gardner, Howard. Leading Minds, 1996, Basic Books
George, Bill. True North, 2007, Jossey-Bass
Kouzes, Jim and Barry Posner. The Leadership Challenge, 2007, Jossey-Bass
Liu, Lan. Conversations on Leadership, 2010, Jossey-Bass
Pink, Daniel. Drive, 2009, Penguin Group
Szollose, Brad. Liquid Leadership, 2011, Greenleaf Books
Senge, Peter. The Fifth Discipline, 2006, Doubleday
Tichy, Noel. The Leadership Engine, 2005, Collins Business
Harvard Business Essentials: Manager's Toolkit, 2004, Harvard Business School Publishing

Made in the USA
Lexington, KY
26 June 2013